START & RUN A MEETING & EVENT PLANNING BUSINESS

Shannon Marie Lach

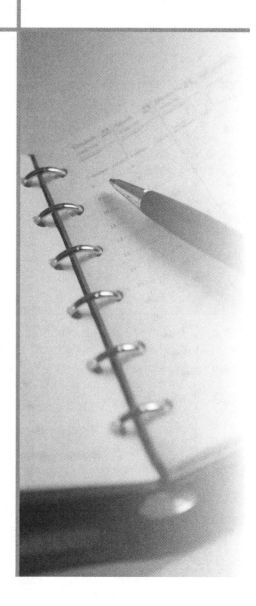

Self-Counsel Press
(a division of)
International Self-Counsel Press Ltd.
USA   Canada

Self-Counsel Press acknowledges the financial support of the Government of Canada through the Canada Book Fund (CBF) for our publishing activities.

Printed in Canada.

First edition: 2014

Library and Archives Canada Cataloguing in Publication

Lach, Shannon Marie, author
    Start & run a meeting & event planning business / Shannon Marie Lach.

Issued in print and electronic formats.

ISBN 978-1-77040-185-3 (pbk.). — ISBN 978-1-77040-954-5 (epub). —
ISBN 978-1-77040-955-2 (kindle)

    1. Special events—Planning—Handbooks, manuals, etc. 2. Meetings—Planning—Handbooks, manuals, etc. 3. Special events industry—Vocational guidance—Handbooks, manuals, etc. I. Title. II. Title: Start and run a meeting and event planning business.

| GT3405.L33 2014 | 394.2068 | C2014-905069-0 |
| | | C2014-905070-4 |

Quote by Tammy Lee Papia, Heavenlee Weddings, used with permission.
Quote by Cindy Ormond, Ormond Entertainment, used with permission.
Quote by Marie Kaminski, Magnolia Events, used with permission.
Quote by Emilee Okon, used with permission.
Quote by Alicia Graser, William's Florist & Gift House, used with permission.

Self-Counsel Press
(a division of)
International Self-Counsel Press Ltd.

| Bellingham, WA | North Vancouver, BC |
| USA | Canada |

START & RUN A MEETING &
EVENT PLANNING BUSINESS

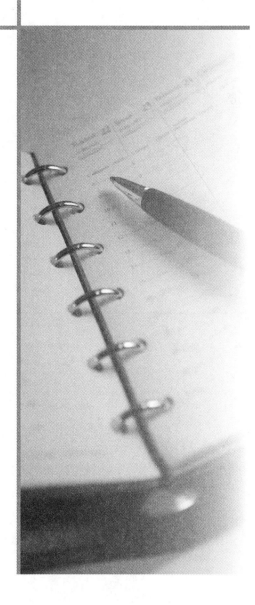

CONTENTS

NOTICE TO READERS

Laws are constantly changing. Every effort is made to keep this publication as current as possible. However, the author, the publisher, and the vendor of this book make no representations or warranties regarding the outcome or the use to which the information in this book is put and are not assuming any liability for any claims, losses, or damages arising out of the use of this book. The reader should not rely on the author or the publisher of this book for any professional advice. Please be sure that you have the most recent edition.

DEDICATION

This book is dedicated to the 750+ event-industry businesses that never returned my inquiries about job applications, sent résumés, or internships. Thank you for allowing me to save all my creativity for PEAR.

I must say, writing this book was much more enjoyable than writing all those cover letters.

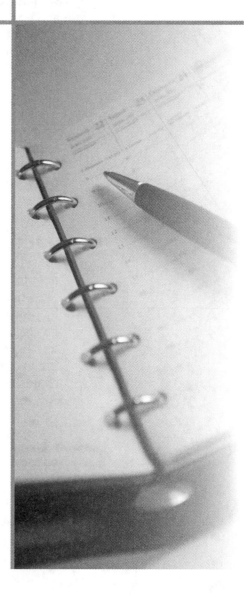

SO YOU WANT TO BE AN EVENT PLANNER

If you want to be an event planner, this book is for you. In this chapter I will discuss how I ended up an event planner and what the life of an event planner is really like.

1. Why Read This Book?

There are three things you should ask yourself before reading this book about meeting and event planning:

- Do I want to build an event planning job as an individual only or do I want to build an event planning company?

- Do I want to expand my business to other areas or cities, and states or provinces?

- Do I mind working weekends and holidays?

If you can answer yes to these questions then this book is for you. This is about creating a company that will influence and produce events on a grand scale. If you are striving to start a part-time event planning career, there is still a need for your services, but this book will walk you through the steps to creating a potentially influential and desirable company.

2. Who Am I?

Everyone: "What do you want to be when you grow up?"

Me: "An event planner."

Everyone: "Ha, good luck. EVERYONE wants to be an event planner!"

Me: "That is OK, I don't care if there are 1 million of them, as long as I am the best!"

As an event planner, the number one struggle is getting into and getting known in the industry. I knew at a very young age that I wanted to be an event planner. I was lucky enough (as an over-achiever, of course) to plan my junior and senior proms. I knew at those moments that this was exactly what I wanted to do for the rest of my life. Little did I know no one else would believe I could. Again, if there are 1 million event planners that is OK, as long as I am the best! This is my story; this is what I do. Your story should be different, but the point is to recognize it. Recognize you have a story worth sharing!

At age 13 I told my mom I would marry my job before I marry a man. Done. Checkmark. (Now I'm waiting for the man. Hello, where are you?)

It may have been this comment at a young age that led my parents to get my IQ tested, and I scored above average, at a genius level. The counselor told my mom, "This girl will become president someday." I won't lie, I did strive to become the first female president for about four months, but then in college, I realized I did not like politics and I could influence people in a more positive fashion by providing them something that I was not able to have (such as giving them the wedding of their dreams, even if I wasn't going to have one, at least right away). Plus I didn't like the idea of living in a white house, I wanted to live somewhere with a bit more character and color!

Ever since I could work I have been working. At 12 I started delivering newspapers and on my 16th birthday I applied for my first job. Often I have held two to four jobs at one time; it was my lifestyle to work from 5:00 a.m. until 10:00 p.m., even in high school.

You name it, I've done it: I've been a lifeguard, worked retail and at a lawyer's office, in food sales, as a marketing coordinator, worked radio, made radio commercials, did promotions for businesses, was a dog walker, was an office manager, worked at a medical school, served and bartended since I was 18 years old, worked for the college I attended, and sold magazine advertising. I have held more than seven internships at various employers', was an executive assistant, worked in the travel department at a corporate office, and even was a model for haircutting experiments.

Everything I did from the age of 17 was the prime reason for me opening my own business. I knew that this was exactly what I wanted to do and what I would do, and I worked my butt off for more than ten years to get where I am today. I paid my dues. Don't get me wrong, I am humbled to be where I am today because I did pay my dues. I did inventory and got my boss coffee and stuffed envelopes for hours to get where I am today. I knew that each moment and each experience was going to lead to a more established business in the end. I firmly believe that I cannot tell somebody to do something unless I have done it myself so I was sure to experience business from every aspect possible and do anything that was asked of me. Well, thought I did everything that was asked of me.

I learned at a very early age I have a problem with authority. I noticed it when I was in high school and had a problem with my coaches on my sports teams. Both my volleyball and basketball coaches "didn't know what they were doing" and apparently I thought I knew better. I'm not sure if my struggle with authority came from my parents, because my father and mother are so supportive and demanding of my capabilities. I think this stern aversion for being told what to do is the main reason I knew I had to open my own business. Yet, I will say, now that I own my business, I don't think it was only about not liking being told what to do, rather it was also about having to answer to only myself.

My love for event planning boils down to the fact that I am accountable for an entire project. My ability to control a project and properly and politely manage individuals and the expectations they are given, has led me to become one of the most influential event planners in upstate New York and hopefully I can continue on to be the most influential event planner in this nation. I am continually flattered by the kind words and admiration toward me that I experience because of my job as an event planner.

However, if I am being completely honest, who I am as a business owner and woman is completely different from who I am when I am home and among friends. I'm actually quite shy and do not enjoy large social settings. I often joke with friends when they ask me to go to a concert or a festival that I only enjoy being in crowds when I am in charge of them.

Don't get me wrong, in my college years I loved to go to parties and I enjoyed being around everyone and socializing, but as I matured and focused on my career I realized that what matters most is what I think about myself, not necessarily what the masses think of me. If I'm happy and proud in what I do, then I can never have a bad day. Just like most actors or performers will tell you they have stage fright and they don't like crowds; once we are put in front of the crowd something changes, we become our "Second Selves," and in the moment we perform. It's our job. We have to. We love to. We want to. Because we have a passion for it. This is what we were born to do.

Within the more than ten years of me working on this business, I have sent out more than 750 applications and résumés to potential event planning firms and marketing positions where events are part of the job. I only heard back from one and that was because I had met an individual at a party who worked at that company. Though I was eventually offered the position I realized that I still couldn't work for somebody else. Let's face it: Who really wants to work for "The Man"?

I never gave up. I continuously tried to contact event firms throughout the nation as well as make local connections with people who could possibly get me a interview or meeting with somebody who was involved in the event industry.

As I mentioned before, entering into the event industry specifically and directly is hard in a small town; well, in any town. Luckily for me my sister had become a wedding photographer and was attending local bridal shows where the event vendors and companies came together to give brides and potential clients a quick look at the services they provide.

At this point my sister and I were not very close nor did we know much about each other. At one of the shows she approached the company that clearly was an event firm in her city. She asked a curly haired, bubbly wedding planner if her sister (me) could potentially came and meet with her about how to get started in the event industry. Without hesitation, the curly haired girl, Katie, said, "Yes, absolutely."

My sister emailed me immediately with the contact name for this individual and was excited for me to have a lead.

I am sure you can guess exactly what I did at that moment. Absolutely nothing. Yep, I did nothing. I don't know if it was fear, but I never contacted Katie.

A few months later my sister emailed me saying, "Hey, have you contacted Katie?" I lied and said yes. I didn't know what else to say because I was so scared of the fact that I knew this one phone call or meeting could change my life forever. Well, my sister was smarter than I thought. She told me that they just went to another bridal show and Katie was there, three months later, and immediately approached my sister and said, "Hey, I never heard from your sister, but I would still love to chat with her if she's interested in learning about the event industry."

That was my sign. I could not believe that katie had remembered speaking with my sister three months earlier. I was beyond shocked that someone actually wanted to help someone in this industry. I knew at that moment that I had to contact Katie and set up a meeting with her immediately.

I did. We met. Being an educated woman with a business background I knew that the best thing to do was maintain a business connection. Actually, the education and business background have nothing to do with it. It's smart to maintain a relationship with anybody you meet that you like.

Katie was kind enough to introduce me to her boss. The first thing I thought of when I left that meeting was, "How do I maintain this connection — this amazing, rare connection — with an event-industry business owner?"

Of course I knew the answer: Work for free. I offered to come in and shadow the company every single weekend for three hours in the showroom, to get experience and exposure into the events industry.

I lived an hour and a half away from the company, so each Saturday I would drive an hour and a half one way to stay there for three hours to get experience and learn, and then drive back home an hour and a half, just to be at my restaurant serving job until midnight. And I did this all for free. Well, technically, not with pay, but I was paid in experience and potential for the future!

As you probably guessed, it paid off. A part-time employee who worked there had attended the same college as I did. She emailed me a few weeks into my shadowing experience and said that a corporate event planner position had opened up in the company and she was sending in my résumé because she knew the effort I was putting in to gain experience in the industry, and was impressed with my dedication.

I was floored that my dreams might be coming true right before my eyes and I hadn't even asked for it.

The interview process went on for about three months and I was pretty sure that I was not going to get the position. In the meantime things were going well at my current job. It was a Friday evening and I was brought into my current employer's office to be told I was given a raise and better position. All I needed to do was go online and fill out the forms to accept the position.

There was still hope that I was going to get the event planning job in the other city so, of course, I didn't fill out the forms that evening, not only because of that but also my family was going on our first trip together for two weeks to Las Vegas. My cousin was getting married there so we made it an entire family affair with cousins and all; it was something that we had never done and we were all looking forward to it. It was monumental. It was a once-in-a-lifetime experience I had to take because it would never come again and nothing could make it better.

I was wrong.

The moment our plane touched down in Las Vegas I had one voicemail, which changed my life. In middle of the airport I cried louder, longer, harder, and deeper than I ever have in my entire life. The voicemail was from the employer at the event firm. I got the job.

Everything I had worked so hard for paid off. This was a dream. My mom and my dad looked at me and they started crying because they knew how much this meant to me.

My passion paid off. I never gave up, and I never would. I couldn't believe this happened and what was going to happen.

Once I returned from Vegas I gave my two weeks' notice to the other company and moved in with my sister and start work at the event firm. Although I had been doing corporate events for the past seven years — that was the position I applied for and was hired for — they told me that day that I would actually be running the wedding and social division.

What, weddings? I never dreamed of getting married and considered my "ideal" wedding, so I wondered how I was going to do this. Instant flashback to me telling my mom I would marry my job before I married a man!

But, I jumped into it and realized that even though I didn't choose weddings, they chose me.

The connections and business colleagues I have met through the wedding industry are irreplaceable; the support and the creative personalities that are found in this industry are priceless.

I realized that I could do weddings and I was really good at them. I have since proven that I'm actually great at them and I believe the reason is because I look at an event like a job. My number one priority is my clients. I want the best for them and I will not impose my beliefs of what a wedding day or event should be on them. I want them to be authentic and reflect their ideas and vision.

I love events, I love what I do, and I've always wanted to be an event planner. I have passion about what I do and what I believe, which is to create a timeless and unique event; this is why I have been so successful and will continue to be.

As we all know, life happens, and things change. Eventually I realized that I wanted to be close to my family and move back home. This prompted me to do a rigorous six-month self-discovery plan and decide what was really going to make me happy was owning my own business.

As with all of my work experiences and connections, I am forever in debt for what I learned at the event firm. If it wasn't for that position I would not be standing where I am today, the owner of PEAR, a successful event planning company.

So I packed my things, moved back home, and started the business plan process with $50 and a website.

2.1 What is PEAR?

People hire my company because they want the experience of being a PEAR client. I want my clients to feel like they are part of an exclusive club. My clients are ones who want the experience of working with us versus just wanting a planner in general. We have created a specific brand. We are known for the caliber of event we produce. We focus on tasteful design, precision timing, and flawless execution. Those who work with us know the excellent service that they will receive when they hire us.

Event planning is a very competitive industry. If you do not think that you can be competitive and proud of what you're producing then it may not be the right choice for you. Great event planners will be challenged and questioned by those around them in a positive way whether it be by other vendors, their clients, or their friends and family. If you're doing something right, you will most likely have to be proud and defend what you are doing. Most people are resistant to change so if you can change the way somebody thinks about event planning, you're doing something right. This is the intention I went into my business with and I maintain it every day.

The first step to creating an event planning company is to think about whether you want to be local, national, or global. This will help you decide on your business plan model as well as your business name. If you want to be local and have no intention of ever wanting to sell the business, you can incorporate your name into the event planning company (e.g., Shannon Lach Events).

If you want your company to be branded and sold nationally or globally, you will likely want to choose a name that seems approachable and is easily recognizable, without your name (e.g., Planning Events & Receptions).

When I was creating PEAR I had three criteria that needed to be part of my business:

1. It needed to be a name I could sell.

2. My name should not be involved with it at all.

3. I should create a logo that people would recognize as belonging to my company.

I also wanted to create an awareness that our company does things a little bit differently than most, so I drew a black pear with a red stem, I chose the alternative to a green pear which people assume would be the obvious choice. It also works in my favor because as I launched my wedding planning division people associated the word PEAR, the fruit, with "pair," as in a couple of people, so PEAR works as a great name for what I do.

I wanted my business name to have a story, and it worked out because my company was named during a Thanksgiving dinner around my closest family; the idea actually came from my brother-in-law; my father, my sister, and my mother were there as well.

The most successful businesses are those that have a story to which people can relate. Whether it's a combination of the partners' names, a street that you grew up on, the name of your favorite cartoon character, or even an acronym for the business partners' names, it's nice to have a story to relate to when speaking with your clients and other potential business owners. I am often asked, "How did you come up with that name?" I explain that PEAR means "Planning Events & Receptions."

I researched the large brands in the world and noticed that they had logos, such as Nike, Reebok, and Apple. So I tried to do the same.

What keeps me doing what I do? I LOVE it!

— *Marie Kaminski,* Event Manager, Magnolia Events

3. Who Are You?

Event planners are reasonably independent individuals. They like the role of creating an identity and being responsible for it. In short, they like to be in control.

With that assumption, this book focuses on someone like you, since you are reading this book. You are educated, creative, and motivated. You like to be in control.

It also assumes that if you are intending to start your own event planning business, you have already accumulated valuable time and experience in the field and think you can offer the event industry something it is missing, something new and profound.

Good for you. We need more innovators in this industry.

If you do not have significant field experience, put this book down, expose yourself to a year of event planning, and then pick up this book again.

A successful event planner who wants to open his or her own venture needs to be passionate about the process and have experience in the field. Having experienced the highs and lows of this job produces an appreciation and passion for what it means to be an event planner.

This job is not about making things look pretty, it is about changing the lives of those who attend the events. You want the clients to have an experience that they have never had before. It is about acknowledging the purpose of an event, and infusing it into the process.

There are a few things you should know going into event planning and one of them is that you will be required to work weekends and holidays. This is something you shouldn't mind as it provides an alternative lifestyle and planning your daily activities in a unique way.

I'm off days when the rest of the world is busy at work. One of the things I love about working weekends is that my days off are generally Sunday and Monday. The best thing in the world is going to the grocery store and having no line at the cashier. It may seem like a trade-off, and it definitely is.

In today's world it's all about making a work schedule that works best for you. Being able to work weekends allows you to make alternative schedules during the week to fill your needs for friends, family, and vacations. A benefit of owning your own company is that you do make your own schedule. If there is an important event, such as your nephew's first birthday, be sure that you do not accept any work events on that weekend. You own the business, you're allowed to allocate your time and make a work-life balance that fits your needs.

Some may argue that you should never turn down money, but I argue that you should never turn down what makes you happy. If spending time with friends and family makes you happy then make a plan and stick to it. Plan your life just like you plan your clients' events.

A harsh reality I learned during my career is that major holidays are potential weekends during which you will not have time off, such as Labor Day, Memorial Day, Fourth of July, and Christmas. I have made it possible by planning something special with my friends and loved ones a day or two before or after the recognized holiday. An example of altering my lifestyle to fit the schedule of an event planner, would be my 30th birthday. I had a wedding job out of town and was unable to celebrate my birthday with friends and family on my actual birthday. I scheduled an intimate dinner at a private club for my closest friends and loved ones to share in the celebration a few weeks later. I am OK with that lifestyle. I chose this, I knew this was a caveat starting the business, and to be happy as an event planner, you have to be OK with this kind of compromise as well.

Joy comes in seeing somebody else's event be perfect. The best gift is knowing you help put a smile on someone's face and made his or her event experience unforgettable. You have to find joy in that and realize that spending your time on a designated holiday to make somebody else's special occasion fantastic is worth the sacrifice.

The day of experience is something that I adore most. I love the stress of having to answer questions, be 17 places at one time, and be accountable for everything that is happening. These exciting moments outshine working on a holiday or weekend.

I thrive under stress, but at the end the success story of the event is worth everything I sacrifice. The success is measured in a happy client, a unique experience for all the guests, and word-of-mouth advertising resulting in a good reputation and more business.

I approach every event as if each person attending is a potential client. This is nonnegotiable; you should always assume everyone in the room could possibly hire you at some point in their life.

Since we have established your true desires and intent on purchasing this book, I have dissected and opened my business process to all of you in hopes that it will inspire the event planners of the future. If you are still passionate about opening your own event firm after knowing it is not fancy and glamorous, please continue reading, you are in the right place.

I have tried to make the process as streamlined as possible to guide you on the path to starting a successful venture. After all, time is money, especially for a service-based career, like event planning.

PASSION. I feel that in order to be successful in the event planning industry, or any industry for that matter, you have to be passionate about what you do!

— *Marie Kaminski,* Event Manager, Magnolia Events

4. Truths and Misconceptions about Event Planners

These are a few truths about entering the event planning industry you must understand before opening your business:

- Your reputation defines you.

- It is a referral-based business.

- Who you know gets you the meeting, what you do gets you the job.

- There are no "normal" working hours.

- Your life will be continuously planned out as much as two years ahead of time for life.

- This is a job, a career, and for you to succeed, it needs to be treated as such.

- You will probably end up spending money you didn't know you had or don't have.

- Your ultimate success will be determined by your ability to handle stress.

- The average time to plan one event is 8 to 16 months.

- Many of your days will be filled with meetings and answering emails.

- In my opinion, you will need to take up yoga before you start your business, and learn how to meditate.

- The work is not pretty, fun, or easy all of the time, but the end result is usually awesome.

Also, consider the misconceptions about the event planning industry:

- You are not Jennifer Lopez, and Matthew McConaughey is not your future husband, like in that movie, *The Wedding Planner*.

- It is not cool in real life to wear a fanny pack filled with safety pins and Band-Aids, but it is your job to do so.

- You don't need professional credentials such as Certified Meeting Planner (CMP) or Certified Special Events Professional (CSEP), but it helps to have them if clients ask.

- We are not "party" planners; we are "event" planners.

- Events can be planned in one month, but make sure your clients realize it won't be cheap!

5. Day and a Week in the Life of an Event Planner

Actual day of an event planner (inside the mind of an event entrepreneur):

Monday

7:00 a.m.

Get up. Sort of.

Play games on phone. Check messages.

Think about getting coffee.

8:00 a.m.

Oh no! That was an hour that went by. OK, really getting up this time, even though I feel like a comfy burrito in my soft bed.

Hmm … I love sleep.

But I have so much work to do!

I guess I will get some coffee.

I wonder if my bride got back to me, she probably didn't like the sample invite I sent her.

I hope my corporate client sets a date for my event pitch, it has been four months since they asked me, and the event is only … oh, three months away … no big deal, not like it is a lot of work to do a corporate event.

Why does it take so long for coffee to brew?

When I am a rich and famous event planner I am going to have a private chef who will make me espresso every morning and have a wonderful dish of fresh fruit and eggs ready for me.

I can lie down for the three more minutes it is going to take the coffee to brew, right?

NO! Be productive. You've got this!

Do I feel like creamer in my coffee, or just sugar? So many calories in sugar but my coffee isn't as good as a Starbucks black coffee, so I guess I need the sugar. Why is my black coffee so awful? Starbucks should give lessons on how to brew coffee … hmm … business idea.

Ah! OK, back to work.

Ugh, I hope the bride liked the invites! I spent three hours searching for a vendor that creates organic, vegan, repurposed invitations with custom silk bows on them. She is going to hate them.

8:15 a.m.

Computer start up

OH MY GOSH! Why is Outlook taking so long to load? This is so cutting into my work time, I already forgot four things I need to do.

Maybe I can nap while it boots up.

No, wait! I see a … nope, still loading.

8:16 a.m.

I really need to go to the gym.

Why can't I be like those other business owners who wake up at 4:00 a.m., eat, go to the gym, shower, read the paper, feed the animals, and go shopping?

OK, thank you computer. Nope, still loading.

8:19 a.m.

Seriously, I need another cup of coffee.

So many files, where do I start?

I need music, now … come on computer, give me Pandora!

Finally! Thank you.

8:20 a.m.

"You've got mail."

Twelve emails, not bad.

Send/receiving 12 out of 204.

No! 150 are spam, and the other 50 are email blasts from Facebook about a new update.

8:30 a.m.

Work, work, work.

9:30 a.m.

I am hungry.

Ugh, why can I never find a good Pandora station?

9:45 a.m.

Work, work, work.

Oh Facebook, I am going to share this!

Work, work, work.

11:00 a.m.

So hungry, and drinking cold coffee.

I really need to start drinking more water and bringing snacks to my desk.

Maybe I will make lunch. I need a break.

4:00 p.m.

Oops. I fell asleep and never ate.

Did I miss a meeting?

It is OK, I can check my emails tomorrow.

Well, let me just check my phone to see if I had any emails.

Oh, just more newsletters.

The bride loved the invite, score! I deserve the night off and Chinese food and ice cream.

Then I am going to spend the night updating my website and new marketing material!

7:00 p.m.

Oh no, that Chinese food and ice cream was such a bad idea.

8:00 p.m.

I am going to spend the night updating my website and new marketing material.

Oh, but *The Voice* is on.

So, not updating my website, but I will bring my laptop on the couch and attempt some work, then end up on Facebook.

I will wake up at 6:00 a.m. tomorrow to get an early start on my website.

All my clients are on track with their planning, it is OK if I take a night to myself to relax and enjoy some reality TV.

9:00 p.m.

I have so much work to do, I should be doing it.

OK, just one more hour then to bed early and up early!

10:00 p.m.

How I Met Your Mother is on after *The Voice*! I have to watch this, it is my favorite.

10:30 p.m.

Darn, my laptop battery died. I could plug it in, but then I would have to go back into the office.

I'll just work on the marketing material tomorrow when I get up at 6:00 a.m.!

Oh, another episode of *How I Met Your Mother*. Watching it.

11:00 p.m.

Bed, here I am!

11:30 p.m.

Why am I still up? Guess I will play a game on my phone.

12:00 a.m.

Candy Crush, I will beat you!

12:30 a.m.

Darn you, Candy Crush!

1:00 a.m.

You win, Candy Crush, good night.

I am kind of hungry again.

I never checked my schedule for tomorrow but I am sure I have no appointments.

There is so much work I have to do that isn't done, what was I doing watching TV instead of working on updating my business plan and employee handbook?

I'll get to it tomorrow.

Tuesday through Thursday

Repeat.

Friday

7 a.m.

SHOOT! Work. I knew I should have done this earlier this week.

8:00 a.m. to 8:00 p.m.

Work, work, work.

At the end of the day, all of the passion you have for the work, work, work fills your life with meaning and love. The moments you create for your couples and clients is irreplaceable. You are a superstar, and you just proved it!

6. Rules for Event Planners

- Be honest.

- Be humble.

- Be fair.

- Be resilient.

- Be creative.

- Be proud.

- Be consistent.

- Be resourceful.

- Be kind.

- Be you.

[Our mission?] Serve our clients with the highest level of integrity.

— *Tammy Lee Papia,* Heavenlee Weddings

7. Start-up Tasks

When starting up, there are a lot of things to do to get your event planning business off the ground. See Checklist 1 for a list of things to consider, and keep reading this book for further explanations of the tools that you will need as you begin working on your business. Checklist 1 is also available in the download kit so you can print and alter it as needed for your business.

CHECKLIST 1
START-UP CHECKLIST

Get a mentor and some experience:

    [　] Local Small-Business Association.

    [　] Event planner from a different state.

    [　] Internships, or shadow for free.

Create a business plan, and a financial plan for a year:

    [　] Personal investment? Do you need loans?

    [　] Create a business name and branding (and test it, and retest it).

Create a reasonable time commitment schedule to work on the business:

    [　] Months 1–6: 20 hours a week.

    [　] Months 7–12: 25 hours a week.

Consult experts as needed:

    [　] Find an accountant or a bookkeeper to help with financials.

    [　] Find a lawyer to help create or look over your contracts for vendors and clients.

Marketing:

    [　] Set up business cards, website, social media platforms.

    [　] Attend tradeshows such as bridal shows.

    [　] Send launch letters to potential partners and clients.

Networking:

    [　] Attend local meet-ups.

    [　] Join the Chamber of Commerce.

Promotional gigs:

    [　] Organize a vendor gathering to meet and greet local vendors.

    [　] Create mini-style shoots for portfolios and networking.

    [　] Throw a free party at which you can practice your event planning skills and get local vendors involved to promote and double as networking. (Hint: They usually will provide items or service for free if they are recognized. Win for everyone!).

Follow-up:

    [　] Send thank-yous to party attendees.

    [　] Always give credit to participating vendors.

Maintain your reputation:

[   ]   Respect everyone.

[   ]   Be gracious.

[   ]   Provide the best service at the highest quality your skills allow.

Maintain connections:

[   ]   Each desired member of your vendor team should be contacted by your company three to five times a year so you stay relevant in their minds.

[   ]   Send an introductory email to everyone you receive a business card from within 24 hours of first meeting.

[   ]   Send a thank-you note within one month following a scheduled meeting or meet and greet.

[   ]   Occasionally stop in unexpectedly with a gift, if they own a shop or store space.

2

TYPES OF PLANNERS

Now that you have decided you want to be an event planner and your chosen career path is exciting to you, it's time to decide what type of event planning position you want. It is rarely addressed that there are three kinds of event planners and it is important that you differentiate between them and decide which one you want to be. There is production, planning, and design elements to event planning. The planning side deals with management, controlling vendors, and setting standards. The design and production elements include creating art and decor as well as possibly holding a warehouse and renting out items.

Figuring out where you want to be will help you decide where you best fit in the industry. Streamline your efforts and find a niche market to grow your business.

1. Types of Event Planners

1.1 Planner

- Enjoys being in charge.

- Enjoys organization at work, not necessarily at home.

- Chances are the Planner doesn't like busy social events when not running them.

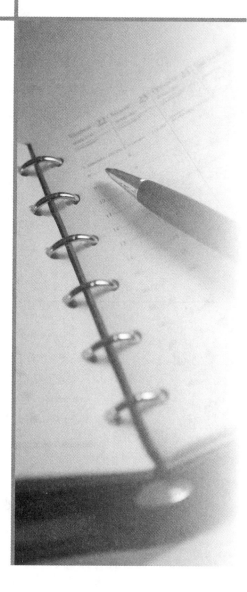

- Influences other people.
- Works well under stress.
- Good interpersonal skills.
- Can delegate.
- Handles autonomy.
- Accountable to a fault and good at holding others accountable.
- Practices effective enforcing.
- Strong problem solver.
- Detail-oriented.
- Takes joy in helping others.
- Seeks and works for the final long-term result.
- Can set and maintain deadlines.

Similar Roles:

- CEOs.
- Executive managers.
- Military officers.
- Detectives.
- Financial advisors.

Possible responsibilities:

- Managing finances.
- Daily networking.
- Meetings and conference attendance.
- Traveling.
- Board membership.
- Enforcing.

1.2 Producer

- Multitasker.
- Action oriented and energetic.

- Can think quick on his or her toes.

- Good salesperson.

- Crafty and handy.

- Likes starting projects, but may not always finish.

- Everything has to have a place.

- Ability to build and run teams.

- Not emotionally attached to the process from start to finish.

- Enjoys immediate gratification.

- Ability to devise quick solutions.

- Certain in his or her decisions.

- Flexible and adaptable.

- Great memory.

- Possible showy personality.

Similar Roles:

- Sales representative.

- Coach.

- Marketing manager.

- Photographer.

- Office manager.

- Personal assistant.

Possible responsibilities:

- Client tracking.

- Manage production team.

- Scheduling.

- Organizing information.

- Manual labor.

- Invoicing.

- Record keeping.

- Purchasing and researching.

1.3 Designer

- Free spirited.
- Works well under direction from others.
- Has personal inspiration he or she wants to share.
- Thought-provoking ideas.
- Prefers a laid-back schedule.
- Enjoys continuous education.
- Volunteers at various organizations.
- Puts others' needs above own.
- Passionate about interests.
- Spontaneous.

Similar Roles:

- Fashion designer.
- Musician.
- Artist.
- Volunteer organizer.
- Environmental ranger.
- Child-care provider.

Possible duties

- Designing sets.
- Requesting samples.
- Drawing and sketching.
- Collaborating with others.
- Conceptualizing a concept.
- Trend watching.

Collaborative versus combative planners: Any planner worth [his or her] salt will have helped pull together a team of event professionals that can be trusted to deliver great results. A planner should work with them and be willing to hear their suggestions … they are the experts in their particular field, after all. You want a planner who is organized, but not completely controlling; preferably someone who is truly a people person.

For example, a planner once sent us a time line that only allowed five minutes for 175 guests to take two small elevators from the first floor cocktail hour to the 20th floor, where the rooftop reception was taking place. Thinking it was a typo, we contacted the planner and learned that not only was it the correct time, but she was completely unwilling to consider our suggestion that the transition would take much longer, affecting the time set for dinner. The night of the event the transition took 40 minutes. Thankfully, we were prepared — in spite of this planner — as was the kitchen staff, thanks to the cooperative relationship between us.

— *Cindy Ormond, Owner,* Ormond Entertainment

FIND YOUR LOCATION, SPACE, AND EQUIPMENT

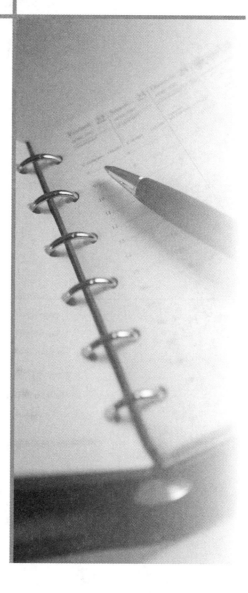

3

1. What Kind of Space Do You Need?

Will you be wanting to use your home office? If so, consider zoning. Sometimes cities are not very welcoming of businesses in homes where there won't be sufficient parking, for example. Or would you prefer a professional building?

Think about the image you wish to portray to clients when deciding on a location.

1.1 Location, location, location

Finding the perfect office location for your business as an event planner can be fairly simple. My first year of business I worked from my home, and my second year of business I worked from a remote office in a professional building, and currently I have an office downtown. My next step is to open a storefront in the suburbs of Buffalo so that I am utilizing my office space as another form of marketing. I will be considering trendy areas, now that my business is at the point where I can afford to do so.

One thing to pay attention to when you don't have an office space outside of your home, is a place where you can potentially meet clients. Ninety percent of my client meetings took place at either a coffee shop or a restaurant in my first year of business. However, this was not ideal. I wanted a space to create an "event environment" so potential clients could experience what I would provide to their special event. What first impression do you want to give your clients? Sometimes clients are traveling from all over your city as well as from different states or provinces. You want to provide them with a location that is suitable for a meeting at any time during the week or weekend. You want a location that expresses your brand.

My three-year goal was to have a building as a storefront so that clients could walk in as well as have meetings there. One of the most important things I knew going into the business was that I needed a physical address for the business. I didn't want to use my home address so I opened a PO Box. I strongly recommend using a PO Box if you start your business in your home. At the beginning of year two I realized that I needed a place where my interns and clients could meet. At this point I had a small budget and was able to move into a professional office complex. This was beneficial since I had somewhere to go to do work. It was professional enough that I could have people meet me there and it was conducive to printing contracts and doing research.

Even though this location was ideal for me at the time and allowed me to have a stationary desk, it was not ideal for reaching out to potential clients. To address this concern, I moved the office into a busy downtown location where young professionals and families lived. This allowed us to use the area and location as additional marketing and advertising since we were able to capitalize on living in a busy area, which gave the business valuable exposure.

We are now in the process of finding a large storefront in a trendy area on a main street surrounded by high-end salons and fashion boutiques. It will be a place at which our people and colleagues can collaborate as well as visit the store.

If you're going to have a physical location for your business, be sure that you have concrete, set office hours. This will allow people to know they can stop in to your business at a moment's notice (during office hours, of course). It also allows for a great meeting place for client proposals.

When your address is visible on your website, you may be seen as more professional. When I worked in marketing research one of the first things I did to assess the professional level of a business was to see if it had a physical address. As I mentioned earlier, if you're unable at first to have a physical location that you can publicize, it is best to at least have a PO Box to receive mail. You do not want individuals showing up to your home if you use your home address as your work address. I strongly recommend you use caution and separate the public address of your business from that of your private home. If you do work from home, I would mention your office location on your website generically, such as only mentioning the city in which you're located. Let individuals know you can meet them at any place throughout that city or town.

Until you have the appropriate funds and the right location, don't skimp on your office because first impressions are just that: first. They can never be done again. Potential clients will judge your business based on your office decor and aesthetics.

Along with every aspect of my business I make sure my office is 100 percent before I launch it or expose it. Throughout the growing process, expectations do change, such as my office location, and what I will settle for in terms of that. As I progress and grow my business I know what my standards are and what I want my clients to think of me when I meet them. I don't settle. Never settle!

Be sure you know your goals for the business as well as your capabilities to execute them. Don't try to overextend yourself. The first one to three years should be about building your brand and making people know that you exist, so not having a physical office location or storefront is completely acceptable if this meets your financial obligations in the first five years.

As I stated at the beginning of this book, I am writing for those who want to build a brand and company, so clearly you would want a location that would allow for employees to work, interns to learn, and potential clients to stop by and ask questions. Obtaining a location like this should be a goal of yours to achieve within five years of starting a business.

When looking at a physical location the first thing I consider is whether or not it has high foot traffic. Our second location downtown was a great area that exposed PEAR to many individuals but the potential for visiting clients was minimal. After our first year, we moved to a place that was more convenient for our clients.

As we look into our next location, we have decided on an area that is closer to the suburbs and located on a main street in a village many people visit and affluent individuals walk the streets each and every day. There's also a drive-by rate of 35,000 cars during the day, giving exposure to our brand. Having a storefront and being visible to the public increases our brand awareness. The dozens of local vendors and businesses surrounding us could be beneficial to us with their support in the event industry.

I'm often asked whether or not there is parking. It seems to be a concern to many people that there is a parking lot or somewhere they can park when visiting. Keep parking in mind when looking for a location.

Selecting an area with high traffic for your business storefront is ideal because you no longer have to spend time and resources educating people about where your business is. If it's a popular main street or village, all you have to do is reference that space in terms of where your business is located. If you have a business off the beaten path or a home office in your garage, chances are you will have to explain to people where it is. A storefront allows people to recognize your name without you even knowing you're trying.

In short, instead of having to say, "We are here," you can say, "Here we are."

Being associated with an affluent and influential area will increase your credibility as a professional and give you higher status. You know you can fit into that community.

There are many ways to find locations available for your business; the first and most effective way I have found is to hit the ground running. Most of the locations I would want my business to be in are locally and privately owned with a "For Rent" sign on the building. These are the places you want to explore instead of expensive real estate listings.

Connecting with your local networking groups and researching on Craigslist may help too. You may be able to find a place from someone you know, so tell people you're looking.

Unless you are intent on purchasing a building, I recommend you rent before purchasing, to gauge the successfulness of your business. In that location be sure you tell the landlords you are using it as an event and wedding planning service location, not a retail store. From there they will be able to tell you if your business is appropriate for their location in terms of zoning and legal issues.

If you do not intend to have a warehouse of rental items and retail goods, most locations should be ideal for your company. If you intend to sell, rent, or have any other items that are of a retail nature, be sure to ask the landlord about zoning and retail policies in the area. You can also connect with a local real estate agent and/or lawyer who may have access to potential buildings and rental properties not listed online or in public knowledge by giving them a hit list of items that you require. Be firm and be aggressive and eventually you will be able to find a place that encompasses your needs and wants, and provides your business the best location for success and growth.

2. What Kind of Equipment Do You Need?

Every office needs equipment so that people can do their jobs efficiently and properly. In my experience, there are the basics and then there are some things that are above and beyond depending on the type of event planner you are. Here is my list of basic needs, although yours may vary:

- Binders for client files.

- Business card box/holder.

- Calendar.

- Cards and envelopes for different occasions.

- Cell phone.

- Clock.

- Computer, laptop, tablet computer.

- Desk.

- Desktop filing system.

- File cabinet.

- Glue.

- GPS.

- Hole punch.

- Inspiration board.

- Landline.

- Magazine rack.

- Magazine subscriptions.

- Pens, pencils, highlighters.

- Plastic sleeves for binders; easier than punching holes.
- Printer.
- Printer paper and ink.
- Post-It Notes.
- Power strip (surge protector).
- Return address stickers.
- Safe lock box.
- Speakers.
- Software: Planning software, OfficeSuite, FaceTime/Skype, online meeting software.
- Stamps.
- Storage boxes.
- Table (to create).
- Tacks.
- Tape.
- Trash can.
- Water, coffee, tea, candy.
- Whiteboard with erasable markers (or chalkboard with chalk).

BUSINESS PLAN, TEMPLATES, WORKSHEETS, AND OTHER FORMS

4

1. Creating a Business Plan

Creating a business plan is the first step to establishing a credible business. It allows you to work through many of the challenges you may face. It also provides a financial forecast to give to potential investors if you need to apply for a loan. It helps you do a SWOT analysis (where you consider your business's Strengths, Weaknesses, Opportunities, and Threats), and allows you to confirm what your goals and mission statement are.

It is integral to have a business plan as a point of reference as your business continues to grow and change. It is a reference tool that you can use as you go deeper into your business and potentially forget your original intentions.

You should write your mission statement last. You want to build your business plan before creating your mission statement because it summarizes what you have in your business plan.

On average you should plan for at least six months to create a fully functional business plan. Be sure to have it reviewed by a local business administration office as well as an individual who is not invested in your business, for a non-biased opinion.

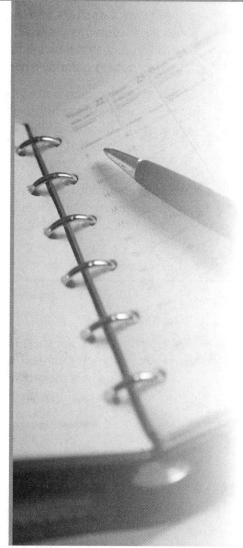

Be prepared to take criticism and advice, because the goal is to create a plan that is easily understandable to any investor, financier, or partner to whom you may potentially give it. Some organizations that are certified in event planning and wedding planning will require a copy of your business plan for your dealings with them.

I have spent many years tracking down and creating the best business plan template for what I think is an all-inclusive business plan. There are also one-page business plan templates on the Web that will help you get started. You can contact your local small-business association office to get business plan advice as well.

I have found that the business plan template in Sample 1 is the best for all the businesses I have created one for; it reminds me of items I may not realize I need to include, as well as allows for the opportunity to change it to fit the specific business I am planning. It is also available in the download kit included with this book.

Read through the sections and the descriptions of what should be included, on the sample. To forecast your financials and calculate start-up costs, see Chapter 5. Finish reading this book, and then start drafting!

1.1 Set Goals

Set your standards in your business plan so that you can maintain them.

The purpose of writing business goals from day one is to create an expectation for your business and streamline your priorities. It is not required that you complete all of these goals immediately, but looking back at what you wanted originally a few years later may help you refocus your vision of the company.

This happened to me when I recently revisited my original goals for PEAR; seeing what I had originally wanted to accomplish brought my focus back to what goals were important to me from the beginning. My original goals reminded me why I started my business and they showed me how much the business has grown.

Here is a sample of goals PEAR had from inception:

April 2012

- Five employees in five years.

- Successful blog created.

BUSINESS PLAN

This template is a starting point for you to create your event planning business plan. It is important you begin this process well before launching your business. Write your mission statement last, as it needs to encompass the whole idea for your business and will be easier to write when you have thought the rest through.

Think through and fill in each section for your business.

Owners:

Your Name: _____

Address 1: _____

Address 2: _____

City, State/Province, Zip Code/Postal Code: _____

Phone Number: _____

Email: _____

Name of Company: _____

Projected Start Date: _____

Business Number or Employer Identification Number (if available): _____

Mission Statement:

Write this section last. Make it a short and sweet snapshot of the business explaining who you will sell to, your role, where you will sell services, what will spell success to you, why people should hire you, and how you will sell your services to clients.

Vision Statement and Company Description:

This is a broad and inspirational statement that discusses size, structure, and influence of your business in the future: Your vision for the company. Think about the following:

- *Who is involved and what experience do they bring to this venture?*
- *What market will you serve in the industry?*
- *What changes do you foresee for your industry in the long and short term?*
- *Where do you see your business in five years? Ten years?*
- *When do you plan on expanding?*
- *Why does your industry need another business?*
- *How do you measure success in your business?*
- *How will your business deal with growth and change?*

Structure and Management:

Think about whether your company is to be a sole proprietorship/partnership/corporation providing wedding, event, and meeting planning and coordination services to local and regional individuals, families, communities, and businesses. Who will be your accountant, board members, banker, insurance agent, mentors?

- *Who will be employed by the company?*
- *What management style will you practice?*
- *Where will you find the right employees?*
- *When will employees get paid?*
- *Why will you have employees instead of contracted individuals, or vice versa?*
- *How will schedules and procedures be prepared and shared?*

Elevator Speech:

Make this no longer than 60 seconds, mention your business name several times throughout the speech, use visual and descriptive words, and end with a tag line of five to ten words maximum.

Think:

- *Who are your target markets?*
- *What EXACTLY do you do?*
- *Where are the benefits to the client who hires you?*
- *When did you enter the industry?*
- *Why are you superior to your competition?*
- *How do your services make the client's life easier?*

Example:

- *At PEAR, as your event planning consultant, we consider ourselves the "masters of management," planting the seed to celebrate the most cherished moments in life.*
- *YOUR event, YOUR vision. Planned by PEAR. We aim for the best, we believe in the best.*
- *Every Detail.*
- *Every Moment.*
- *PEAR creates and manages private celebrations, business monumental moments, corporate celebrations, and any moment in your life worth celebrating.*
- *Life is a series of events. Let PEAR help you plan them.*
- *Call us today for a free consultation about how we can make your event one-of-a-kind.*
- *PEAR, making every event tasteful.*

Products and Services:

What services will you provide in the next 12 months, how long do you estimate it will take to execute for each element you will offer of your business?

Think about:

- *Who is your target market?*
- *What is your estimated life cycle of services provided?*
- *Where will your services be marketed (have photos, brochures, advertisements, and other in appendix)?*

- *When do you believe your service benefits the client?*
- *How will your service have a competitive advantage or disadvantage in the industry?*

Industry Overview:
- *Who is currently your industry leader and biggest competition, locally and globally?*
- *What are the average pricing structures in your market?*
- *When is your service in demand?*
- *Where is your niche, or unique share in the market?*
- *How will you overcome barriers to entry?*

Marketing Plan:
- *Who is your target market?*
- *What is your sales and promotion strategy?*
- *Where will you brand your company and where will you take it logistically?*
- *When will you implement these plans?*
- *Why are your methods of marketing going to be successful?*
- *How will you brand the company to be recognizable to clients?*

Regulatory Issues:
- *With whom may you need to have nondisclosure agreements?*
- *What requirements does your business structure entail?*
- *Where are there zoning or building requirements?*
- *When are deadlines for applications and regulatory forms?*
- *Why may you not have any regulatory issues?*
- *How many permits and licenses are required for your business to start up?*

Risk Plan:
- *Who will you refer or recommend if you are unable to provide service?*
- *What are potential services you can't provide?*
- *Where will you document failures and your follow-up to these?*
- *When will you determine your business is at risk?*
- *Why do you think your business will ever be at risk?*
- *How will you measure what risks your business is currently facing?*

Operational Plan:
- *Describe your location, equipment, people, processes, and surroundings.*
- *Where will you have your office?*
- *Who will need access to your location?*
- *What will be your structure to monitor quality control?*
- *When will your business be open?*

- *Why did you choose certain equipment and processes?*
- *How will your services be provided to the client?*

Financial Plan:

- *Who is liable for business finances?*
- *What are the personal financial statements of the owners (include in appendix)?*
- *Where do you project your business profit projection to be in 12 months? Two years?*
- *Why did you make the assumptions about projected cash flow?*
- *How will your payment plan affect your cash flow and inventory?*

Start-up Expenses and Plan:

How much do you need for start-up and when does start-up begin and end? Who will front the start up costs and what percentage ownership will he or she hold? What will expenses be? What is your contingency plan?

Investment Plan:

- *Do you have the money or do you need additional financing or loans? Where will you seek the money?*
- *What are your projected sales and expenses? How much profit do you expect?*
- *Where will you open your business bank account?*
- *When will you break even?*

Pricing and Payment:

- *Will you be taking cash, credit, check, PayPal? How and where? Will you be invoicing clients and what will your terms be?*

Appendices:

Include as much of the following as you can to back up what you said throughout the business plan.

- *Brochures and marketing materials including logo.*
- *Personal financial statements.*
- *Start-up cost details.*
- *SWOT analysis.*
- *Photos and maps of office location.*
- *Detailed list of office equipment needed.*
- *Copies of business documents, leases, and contracts.*
- *Industry-related articles that support what you want to do.*
- *Book references to research.*
- *Detailed market research.*
- *Letters of support from past or potential customers.*
- *Letters of referral from colleagues.*
- *Your biography and experience/a résumé.*

- Submit weddings to publications and national blogs.

- Fee structure growth: Pay fee and percentage overall event eventually.

- Create training manual for interns and staff.

- Have vocational trainings for two days and go through events for upcoming year.

- Have training sessions to train staff and gain business connections.

- Commit three years to a specific location in upstate New York.

- Meet minimum sales goals each year.

- Create trademark logo.

- Have a PEAR embossed on both sides of business cards.

- Create monthly checklists with stickers tracking progression.

- PEAR will be a group of planners from which clients can choose the planner who fits his or her personality best. I will streamline clients to meet with the planner I think is best and each planner can have his or her own prices based on expertise.

December 2012

- Create a division called PEARstyle which will product photo shoots every quarter.

- Update website and Facebook.

- Use specific photos to create a simplified vision. In present tense, who we are — be descriptive.

- Research other planners in the area.

- Research great marketing ideas in other cities.

- Quarterly work goal sheet — rate how it went.

- Create a SCRUM form for meetings.

- Put together a Buffalo bridal blog.

- Vision for Buffalo Boutique Bride, an intimate bridal show.

- Google relevant wedding information; possible controversial topics to refute?

- Create PEAR Instagram account.

- Start local group: Company of young creative planners — what's going on — internal and external — case studies — photos of events to share.

- Create spreadsheet tracking progress of social media.

- Find us on Facebook and tell us why; fresh ideas; free gift.

- Facebook giveaway each quarter: For new "likes," everyone who "likes" in a 24-hour period is entered to win.

- Engagement plan: Giveaways for holidays (keep relevant to culture) and donations to family.

Your goals should be all-inclusive, over the top, and excessive. This is the time of your business plan where you can dream big and find out what really drives you as an event planner.

2. Other Templates and Forms

Here is an initial list of templates and forms you may wish to create before you launch your business. It is nice to have standard answers to inquiries, to keep things simple and professional.

2.1 Email template ideas

- Client inquiry.

- Sending a contract.

- Thank-you to a client.

- Refusal of a meeting.

- Refusal of an event.

- Out-of-office reply.

- Job, interview, or internship inquiries.

- Meeting inquires.

2.2 Phone answering and voicemail templates

At PEAR, we use a standard greeting when we answer the phone. We also have rules for our voicemail. See Sample 2.

2.3 Other letters and business worksheets

There are several other types of letters and business tracking worksheets that will come in handy in your business. Consider creating an introductory letter about your company (see Sample 3), a thank-you letter to clients, and a client questionnaire with all of the questions specific to your business and their events. You may also consider creating client tracking programs specific to your type of meeting or event planning business and its clients, and a tracking sheet to track your business connections (which will come in handy). Make sure to consistently brand all of your stationery and anything the public will see.

Something you will need with every event and client is an Event Budget Worksheet to keep costs on target, and see where things are getting out of hand. See Chapter 5, section **4.**, Event Budgeting. The samples shown there are also available in the download kit included with this book so you can modify them for your business.

3. In-house Contracts

You will want to create contracts to have clients and vendors sign, to protect yourself and your business, and to ensure details will be looked after. You should make sure that you have a lawyer look over all of your contracts, but you also want to make sure that your contracts help create an image for your business because this is the first document that clients will receive after they have met with you and another step toward possibly providing services for them. It is a good idea to bring a contract with you to every meeting because your contracts mark the first time that you will be getting a signature, allowing you to start work on a project.

The contract should look pretty, of course, since image is important in this business, but also be descriptive. Bullet points are good because you want to make the stipulations of your contract easy to read and open for discussion if needed.

Be sure that you save every contract you create with the client's name and the date, as well as put it in the header and footer so that there is no confusion. You also want to make sure that you date it from the time that you sent it so that if there are multiple changes you can be sure to use the most updated form.

During the process I always keep any changed contracts, printed and filed after the event. I also save all of my files online and to my hard drive and make a printed copy so that I will have the files on hand for reference in the future if I need them.

SAMPLE 2
PHONE ANSWERING AND VOICEMAIL RULES

How to Answer the Phone at PEAR:

Thank you for calling PEAR. You have reached us while we are either assisting another client or out of the office. Please leave a detailed message including your name, event date, and services required. We will return your call at our earliest convenience. Thank you, and enjoy your day.

Voicemail and Answering Machine Rules:

1. Fifteen seconds to answer.

2. Record from landline to avoid static and interference.

3. No background noise.

4. Be energetic but not overwhelming in your tone.

5. Speak slower than you think you should.

6. Speak more clearly than you think you should.

7. Listen to the message before you approve.

8. Say who they called.

9. Give an explanation for why you didn't answer.

10. Say the next steps they should take.

11. Say what you need from them.

12. Thank them and be kind.

We're happy to introduce the launch of the luxury event planning company, P E A R (Planning Events and Receptions), serving the Upstate New York area. P E A R is a small business that is nimble and effective. Our staff has worked with both large companies and individuals to develop effective solutions to their event planning challenges. P E A R would like to work with you and your clients as well.
Our keen knowledge of the event industry has helped us develop trust and expertise among colleagues, to answer the needs of today's clients. Our expertise will allow you to:

- Increase productivity while we streamline the event planning process.
- Reduce research time for client inquires outside of your scope.
- Rely on us as a liaison between you and your client.
- Be assured all questions are answered correctly and in a timely manner.
- Know the event will run seamlessly and problems will be solved by us.
- Save your clients time and money while adhering to their budget.
- Do what YOU do best and leave the rest up to us!

The entire staff and management are thoroughly professional. They stick to deadlines and deliver quality services. P E A R has gained raving clients and colleagues due to our effective working style and exceptional service.

As part of our introduction to new vendors and partnerships, any clients you refer to us entitle the client to a 10% discount. Should your business needs change over time, we will be more than happy to evaluate these changes to provide the best service that we can. If for any reason we do fall short of your expectations, please do not hesitate to contact us.

You can contact Shannon Marie Lach at 555.555.5555 or shannon@pearplanning.com.

We are looking forward to meeting with you to discuss the possibilities of building a pleasant association in the future!

Sincerely,

Shannon Marie Lach

Always have a backup of all files; your computer can crash, and your files can burn, so be sure that you back up your system or use an online program such as the cloud or Google Drive.

Some contracts that you may want to create (with legal advice) specific to your business include:

- Consultation contract.
- Day of management contract.
- Corporate events contract.
- Social events contract.
- Wedding contract.
- Nonprofit fundraiser contract.
- Model release.
- Photographer release.

An example of a contract I use for destination wedding planning is shown in Sample 4. The one you create will need to be specific to your business, the type of event, and the area in which you operate (consult your lawyer for legalities).

DESTINATION WEDDING CONTRACT

P E A R

PLANNING EVENTS AND RECEPTIONS

www.pearplanning.com
123 Bidwell Parkway, Door 4
Buffalo {New York} 14222
716-512-9166
MyEvent@pearplanning.com

Client Information

Name (client)	
Address	
Phone	
Email	
Date of Event	
Event Location	
Date Prepared	
Payment Due	Upon Signing

Bridal Planning Expectations

I.   Pre-Wedding Communication

- Create, edit, and assist Client in budget planning and adherence to event budget.
- Meet with the client as appropriate or at request of client to discuss details.
- The Bridal Couple (and Mother of the Bride) will have unlimited phone and email access to the Planner at the moment of signed contract until the wedding day.
- Within two weeks of wedding date, set up meeting with client to finalize timeline and collect items needed for ceremony/reception.

II.   Design Consultation

- Provide a design detail consultant to assist in the design elements of your ceremony and reception.
- Design consultation will also include advice, tips, and suggestions for other design details including but not limited to stationery design, room layout, color choices, linen selections, centerpiece ideas, ambient decor, etc.
- Company may use a private Pinterest board or other means to communicate design inspirations to Client.

III.   Service Providers and Vendor Communication

- Provide destination wedding venue and vendor recommendations for both ceremony and reception by sending photos, links, and organized information to include venue guidelines, curfews, deposits, and fees.
- Provide pre-research and recommend the perfect creative partners tailored around the clients preferences and budget until selected; such as invitations, flowers, etc. as well as the following throughout the process:
  - Dress shopping.
  - Menu selection.
  - Wedding etiquette advice.
  - Finding a wedding location.
  - Tipping etiquette advice.
  - Arranging travel and hotel accommodations.
- Schedule preliminary Skype phone meetings with selected vendors and service providers for client and Planner will attend all meetings if capable.
- Client will provide Planner with all contracts and vendor information to be reviewed before signing.
- Planner will communicate directly with each service provider and vendor as an extension of the bridal couple.
- Planner will create a detailed time line of events and share with all service providers, vendors, bridal couple, and bridal party two weeks prior to event.
- A printed time line will be available to all vendors on the day of the wedding.
- Schedule arrival and departure times of all vendors and service providers, as well as guests and bridal party.
- Planner will assist client in room layout and placement of event specs.

IV. **Day of Coordination**
- A Project Planner will:
    i. Direct for an unlimited time on your wedding day.
    ii. Organize and direct the bridal party and family members.
    iii. Oversee all aspects of your wedding day, including but not limited to constant communication with: Baker, Band/DJ, Caterer, Decorator, Florist, Photographer, Transportation, Venue, and Videographer.
    iv. Become the initial point of contact for all service providers and vendors, becoming a liaison for the Bridal Couple, so they may enjoy the day.
    v. Coordinate collection of gifts and cards to the best of their ability and place in a predetermined secure place for the Bridal Couple.
    vi. Distribute any necessary payments due on the event date.
    vii. Be present at your ceremony rehearsal for one hour.
        (It is to be expected a Project Planner is aware of all situations at all times.)

V. **Your Destination Wedding Planner will also provide:**
- Accommodation recommendations.
- Recommendations for group activities the week of your event.

VI. **Required Destination Wedding Planner Terms and Conditions**
- Travel, stay, food and beverage must be provided in full by the client for the Planner, this can include additional costs as discussed with the Client.
- Planner requires arrival time to destination at least 24 hours prior to the rehearsal to check in with vendors and venue.
- Planner will make necessary pre-wedding trips to destination if requested and paid in full by Client.
- Client has access to Planner on the Rehearsal Day and Wedding Day 24 hours if needed.
- Client should acknowledge travel brings possibility of delays, that may affect the service provided by the Planner, and the Planner is not held responsible if the delay is the fault of the transportation system, natural disaster, or other catastrophe beyond the Planner's control. It is understood that should this happen, the Planner will make every effort to inform the client and attempt to remedy the delay at his or her best ability. Any additional fees inferred from this situation will be the sole responsibility of the client.
- Client is responsible for the shipping or delivery of any personal and wedding related items to the destination.

We at PEAR truly look forward to helping you create
your signature wedding with your vision,
your style, and LOVE!

PEAR
PLANNING EVENTS AND RECEPTIONS

www.pearplanning.com
123 Bidwell Parkway, Door 4
Buffalo {New York} 14222
716-512-9166
MyEvent@pearplanning.com

Service Fees {2015}

Services will be provided in correlation with the following fees, upon payment:

Item	Quantity	Cost	Total
Full Event and Wedding Planning	0	$5,000.00	$5,000.00
Event and Wedding Day Directing	0	$1,500.00	Included
Additional Event and Wedding Consulting	0	$75/hour	As needed
Event and Wedding Decor Rentals	0	---	As needed
Extended Travel (cost per mile)	0	$75	As needed
Lodging (required for events 30 miles out of Buffalo)	0	---	As needed
Total			$5,000.00

Payment Schedule

Deposit: Signed Contract and $2,000 Nonrefundable Deposit due at signing

6 months prior: ½ of remaining balance

3 months prior: remaining balance to pay contract in full

A finance fee of 2% will be applied to all unpaid invoices 30 days following the event.

Sincerely,

Shannon Marie Lach

Shannon Marie Lach
Owner, Principal Planner
P E A R

Acceptance of Contract

I, _____ the Client, accept the terms and conditions of this contract in full. I am aware of my financial obligations to pay a fee of 50% of my originally determined cost and will be notified of any changes. By authorizing the contract with my signature, I confirm I wish to hire PEAR for my event, exclusively.

_____   _____
CLIENT SIGNATURE   DATE

Terms and Conditions

1. Additional Costs. It is understood and agreed that **PEAR** (Company) shall have the right on behalf of and in the name of the (Client) understands the Company is to inform Client of all costs concerning additions or changes made the day of event. These include, but are not limited to, additional guests, time extension of event, and all costs involved with extension of event from additional vendors. Client also agrees that all additional costs will be reflected in final invoice and are to be paid in full within 30 days of receiving the final notice as to paragraph 1. Should any additional charges or costs be accrued with any contracting party under paragraph 1 because of a delay in payment by Client, the Client agrees to be responsible for such amounts.

    a. Client must provide up to two night's stay for Planner of Company if event location is 30 miles outside of the Buffalo, New York, city limits so they may provide exceptional service and availability to Client for their rehearsal and event day. A room is required to be booked under the Planner's name with the Client's payment method and a confirmation contract from the hotel at least two weeks prior to the event date.

    b. Gas and mileage costs will be applied if they are outside average scope of service for Planner, and/or additional site visits are required beyond the allotted times in contract.

    c. Client is required to pay all travel and stay expenses for events planned outside of the New York State region, including but not limited to air fare, transportation, lodging, meals, and all included costs.

2. Advances for Payments. Client agrees to provide to the Company, as requested by the Company, necessary amounts of partial payments, deposits, or prepayments for matters needed beyond Company Scope.

3. Liability for Payments upon Cancellations. Client shall be fully liable for all payments hereunder regardless of cancellation or modification of Client's plans as entered into between the parties. Client shall likewise be liable for any cancellation charges or penalties that may occur because of changes of plans by Client.

4. <u>Service Standards</u>. It is understood that the services to be provided by Company hereunder are not subject to a definitive standard and will require the exercises of judgment by Company. To the extent written standards are provided with this contract, the Company shall have the obligation to perform under such. Otherwise, Company shall be entitled to use its reasonable judgment and discretion in the manner of performing services.

5. <u>Taxes</u>. Client agrees to pay, or reimburse Company, for any and all sales and use taxes incurred as a result of performing services under this Agreement.

6. <u>Photography and Social Media</u>. It is understood that the Company will request images from the event photographer to provide images to use in Company Marketing and Social Media campaigns. The Company may also take photos and publish them on social media as promotion.

7. <u>No Additional Services</u>. The parties agree that Company shall incur no additional obligation to perform services hereunder, and Client shall incur no additional obligation to pay Company for services unless such agreement is confirmed in writing.

8. <u>Description of Services</u>. Company will provide client in writing a detailed description of proposed services at least 60 days before delivery. Client will be deemed to have accepted such services as described as satisfying the requirements under this contract unless a written request for change is received within 30 days of scheduled activity.

9. <u>Third-Party Vendors</u>. It is understood that Company in the performance of this agreement is required to contract on behalf of Client with others; Company's responsibility shall be to exercise reasonable judgment in its choices of other contracting parties.

10. <u>Indemnification</u>. Client agrees to indemnify and hold harmless Company from any loss, claim, or expense in relation to this contract, or services under it, except such as arise solely from the negligence of Company.

11. <u>Limitation of Liability</u>. Each party agrees that as a basis for the bargain, and as a factor in determining the contract price, each wishes to limit possible claims. Therefore, Company agrees that for any breach or failure to perform under this contract, of any type or kind, or for any negligence, Company's recovery from Client shall be limited to the contract amount to be paid by Client, any liability and charges assumed by Company under paragraph 1 above, and interest on such amounts as allowed by law. Client agrees that upon any breach of this contract or other claim including negligence arising out of or related to this contract or the services of Company, Client's recovery shall be limited to amounts actually paid to Company, or expended pursuant to paragraph 1 above, for which services were not performed. Each party expressly waives and claims for consequential or resulting damages against the other.

12. <u>Alcoholic Beverages</u>. If the Client has requested the beer, wine, or other alcoholic beverages be served during its activities to which this Purchase Agreement relates, Client understands that Company is not licensed to sell any such beverages and cannot do so as a part of its services. The client acknowledges that Company cannot supervise or control, and is not responsible for actions, omissions, or misconduct of Client's employees, members, agents, guests, or invitees. In addition to any provisions in this Agreement, Client does hereby, specifically, agree to indemnify, hold harmless, and defend Company, its employees, agents, and contractors from any cost, expense, loss, damage, liability, settlement, or judgment incurred by Company, its employees, agents, or contractors, including, without limitation, reasonable attorney fees, expenses, and preparation of litigation, court costs, and the like. This indemnity and hold harmless shall apply to any claim, proceeding, or litigation, asserted against or involving Company, its employees, agents, or contractors, and regardless of by whom made or brought, including, but not limited to, third parties or members of the public. This indemnity and hold harmless shall apply to the extent any such claim, proceeding, or litigation is asserted to involve conduct alleged to have involved, or be caused by, directly or indirectly, in whole or in part, any beer, wine, or other alcoholic beverages, their containers or the serving or consumption of any such beverages.

13. <u>Damage and Conversion</u>. Client understands that many of the decorations, furniture items, serving items, small wares, equipment items, and props are rented for the occasions, or are the property of Company or other contractors. Should any such items be damaged or converted by Client or its employees, agents, or guests, then Client agrees to pay the replacement costs of such items.

14. <u>Choice of Law</u>. This agreement shall be construed as a contract executed and intended to be performed in the State of New York and shall be interpreted under the laws of New York.

15. <u>Entire Agreement</u>. This agreement constitutes the entire agreement of the parties and all prior discussions, negotiations, representations, and warranties are merged herein.

16. <u>Modification</u>. Any modification or amendment of this Agreement must be in writing and must be signed by both the Company and Client.

17. <u>Special Needs/Disabilities</u>. Client will notify the Company if any attendees have any special needs/disabilities so the Company can plan appropriately.

18. <u>Act of God</u>. If, because of any condition arising from a state of war, act of God, force majeure, or other cause beyond the control of the Company, the Company shall deem it advisable to cease, suspend, or reduce the services or any activity provided or scheduled to be provided under this agreement, then the Company shall first be entitled to adequate substitution of such other service or activity. If the Company is unable or unwilling to provide such substitute service or activity then such original services or activity shall be rescheduled to such time as is mutually agreeable to the Company and the Client. In the event that no substitute is available and no agreement is reached on rescheduling, the provisions of the cancellation policy shall apply.

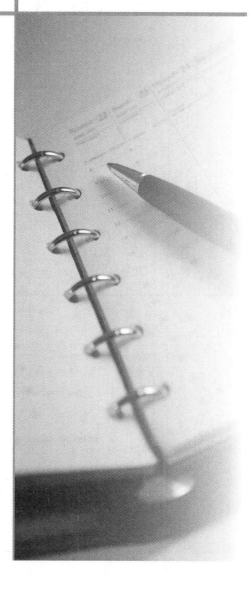

SET YOUR PRICING AND EVENT BUDGETING

5

1. Know Your Costs

Before you can set adequate prices for your services you need to know what your start-up costs will be. Hopefully, you will do this when you are thinking through your business plan. In Sample 5, I have listed some of the things that will be one-time costs, and some of the costs that will be incurred monthly. Consider each item (and any that may be specific to your business that I have not listed). The worksheet is also available in the download kit included with this book so you can alter it when you are figuring out your start-up costs.

2. Pricing

It is important to set your pricing when starting a business so that you have a realistic expectation of what you will make and how much you need to charge. After you do your research of local event planners and see what the average prices for services are, set your prices where you want. It is important to set these price structures prior to opening a business so that you can be confident when you go into a meeting.

I set my price structures at the high end so that vendors and local business owners knew

START-UP COSTS WORKSHEET

START-UP COSTS WORKSHEET FOR SMALL BUSINESS

One-Time Start-up Costs

Item	Qty	Unit	Total	Notes
Building or Retail/Office Space	1	$350.00	$350.00	
Parking	1	$100.00	$100.00	
Office Fixtures				
Bookshelf	2	$489.99	$979.98	Office Max Catalog pg 501
Coffeemaker	1	$200.00	$200.00	Keurig Coffeemaker and Pods and Accents
Coffee Table	2	$229.99	$459.98	OMC pg 601
Couch	2	$899.99	$1,799.98	Office Max Catalog pg 601
Decorations	1	$2,000.00	$2,000.00	
Dishes	1	$200.00	$200.00	Christmas Tree Store 4 sets of dinnerware/mugs/silverware
Food	1	$100.00	$100.00	Random Non-perishibles/Candy
Glasses	10	$5.00	$50.00	Tumblers/Wine Glasses
Lamps	2	$21.99	$43.98	OMC pg 716
Microwave	1	$250.00	$250.00	Home Depot Panasonic Brushed Nickle
Paint	4	$30.00	$120.00	
Refrigerator	1	$200.00	$200.00	Home Depot 4cu Black
Rug	1	$250.00	$250.00	
Silverware	10	$5.00	$50.00	
Sound System	1	$500.00	$500.00	
Store Front Sign	1	$250.00	$250.00	
TV	2	$750.00	$1,500.00	Best Buy 40" Hi Def
TOTAL			$9,403.92	
Office Equipment				
Binders	25	$4.79	$119.75	OMC pg 53 Office Max Double View Red/Black Binders
Camera	1	$500.00	$500.00	Kodak Zoom
Cell Phone	1	$400.00	$400.00	iPhone with Data Plan
Chair	1	$839.99	$839.99	OMC pg 576 Mayline
Computer	1	$4,000.00	$4,000.00	Mac Laptop
Desk	1	$2,000.00	$2,000.00	OMC pg 503
File Cabinet	1	$359.00	$359.00	OMC pg 628 Safco wheels with drawer
File Folders	10	$8.00	$80.00	OMC pg 427 DIVOGA Catherine Folders
File Holders	4	$13.29	$53.16	OMC pg 412 Interlocking Hanging Files
Hole Punch	2	$55.00	$110.00	OMC pg 1040 Swingline Punch
Ink	4	$76.00	$304.00	
iPad	1	$829.00	$829.00	Apple iPad 64 gb
Keyboard Pad/Mouse Pad	1	$59.99	$59.99	OMC pg 308 3M
Lable Maker	1	$89.00	$89.00	DYMO Lable Maker Walmart
WiFi	1	$50.00	$50.00	Verizon with Cell Phone
Paper	2	$35.00	$70.00	OMC pg 824 Office Max Brand All in One

Item	Qty	Unit	Total	Notes
Pens	4	$15.00	$60.00	OMC pg 875 Paper Mate Blue Retractable
Printer	1	$400.00	$400.00	Office Depot - All in One
Scissors	3	$9.00	$27.00	OMC pg 1067 Office Max Red
Sewing Machine	1	$200.00	$200.00	Walmart - Singer Computerized
Shredder	1	$1,250.00	$1,250.00	OMC pg 1076 Fellowes Power Shredder
Stapler	2	$16.39	$32.78	OMC pg 1117 Swingline Classic Red
Telephone	1	$100.00	$100.00	Vintage Dial Phone
OTHER	1	$150.00	$150.00	Misc. Items
TOTAL			$12,083.67	
Wardrobe	1	$1,000.00	$1,000.00	
Conferences	2	$2,000.00	$4,000.00	Event World/ISES
TOTAL			$5,000.00	
Inventory				
7-12" Uprights	4	$100.00	$400.00	http://www.rosebrand.com/product631/Adjustable-Uprights-for-Standard-Pipe-Base-Systems.aspx?cid=185&idx=2&tid=1&info=Standard%2bPipe%2b%2526%2bBase
Bases	4	$40.00	$160.00	http://www.rosebrand.com/product609/Low-Profile-Bases-for-Standard-Pipe-and-Base-Systems.aspx?cid=185&idx=1&tid=1&info=Standard%2bPipe%2b%2526%2bBase
7- 12" Cross Bars	3	$40.00	$120.00	http://www.rosebrand.com/product629/Adjustable-Horizontal-Drape-Supports-for-Standard-Pipe-Base-Systems.aspx?tid=2&info=drape%2bsupport
Pole Pockets		$0.00	$0.00	
TOTAL			$680.00	
Remodeling and Installation	1	$2,000.00	$2,000.00	
Cable/Internet Service	1	$150.00	$150.00	
Telephone Service	1	$50.00	$50.00	
Licenses and Permits				
Lawyer Fee	1	$500.00	$500.00	
Accountant Fee	1	$500.00	$500.00	
Name Registration	1	$50.00	$50.00	
Trademark	1	$1,000.00	$1,000.00	
SCorp	1	$2,500.00	$2,500.00	
TOTAL			$6,750.00	
Branding				
Business Cards	200	$2.00	$400.00	
Graphic Design	1	$450.00	$450.00	
Letterhead	200	$1.50	$300.00	
Promo Flyers	200	$3.00	$600.00	
Thank-You Cards	200	$2.00	$400.00	
Website	1	$1,000.00	$1,000.00	
TOTAL			$3,150.00	
Initial Advertising and Promotions				

Item	Qty	Unit	Amount	Notes
Client Giveaways	1		$300.00	Letter Opener, Bridal Binder, Thank-You PEAR
Client Packages	30	$15.00	$450.00	
Coaster Bar Blitz	1		$300.00	
Grand Opening Party	1		$2,000.00	
Magazine Subscriptions	1		$400.00	Harvard Business Review, Entrepreneur, WellWed, NY Times, INC., Home & Design
Networking	1		$500.00	Chamber of Commerce, Women's Business Organization, Toastmasters
Rochester/Syracuse Wedding Magazine	1		$2,000.00	
The Knot	1		$2,000.00	
WellWed Magazine	1		$2,000.00	
TOTAL			$9,950.00	
Storage Unit	1	$100.00	$100.00	
Car			$0.00	
Cash on Hand	1	$1,500.00	$1,500.00	
Other			$0.00	
TOTAL			$1,600.00	
Total One-time Start-Up Costs:			$48,617.59	

Regular Monthly Expenses			$0.00	
Salaries of Owner/Managers	1	$2,000.00	$2,000.00	
Other Salaries and Wages	1	$3,000.00	$3,000.00	
Rent or Mortgage Payments	1	$350.00	$350.00	
Other Loan Payments	1	$250.00	$250.00	
Goods and Supplies	1	$500.00	$500.00	
Office Expenses	1	$150.00	$150.00	
Maintenance and Repairs	1	$150.00	$150.00	
Distribution and Delivery Charges	1	$200.00	$200.00	
Advertising and Promotional Costs	1	$300.00	$300.00	
Legal and Professional Services	1	$450.00	$450.00	
Utilities and Telephone				
Land Phone	1	$60.00	$60.00	
Cell Phone	1	$150.00	$150.00	
Insurance	1	$350.00	$350.00	
Taxes, including Social Security	1	$250.00	$250.00	
Personal Upkeep	1	$500.00	$500.00	Hair, Nails, Clothing, etc.
Misc. Expenses	1	$300.00	$300.00	
TOTAL			$8,960.00	

what type of services and excellence I was providing. The most important thing is no matter what price structure you use in your business, you make sure that you meet the expectations of your brand. I'm not saying you can't negotiate with clients and offer special promotions and discounts for family and friends, but be sure you maintain the standards that you started the business intending to keep.

Let's be honest: It's all about status and reputation. By letting potential clients know that I have set prices and can meet the standards someone would expect of someone with those prices, it allows my clients to brag that they were able to hire the best in the area. Isn't that what you want for your event? To say you have the best planner and all of your guests were jealous you could do something so extravagant?

It is important to set a price structure for individual clients before you meet them; whether it be a bride or a corporate client make sure you do your research to see what exactly the event entails, and how much time and research you will have to put into it so you can create a potential pricing structure for that exact individual. It is nice to be able to customize services, and clients like to know you have done this for them. If you're stuck on quoting a price that is exactly the same for a bride as it is for a corporate client, you may not be doing yourself any favors, and the client might figure this out and hesitate about whether or not to hire you, since the services provided, although very similar, are also quite different for different types of events.

Stick to your standard pricing if you are meeting with a client and he or she is concerned that your prices are too high. If the client does not understand the value in your services after meeting you, he or she may not be the client for you. Be OK with letting a client walk.

Knowing how I set my fee for the area and that an event planner's work is not completely understood, I met with multiple clients that I provided pricing for and they felt it was too high and they wanted to do the work themselves. After acknowledging their concerns were valid, if they still were not interested in working with us, it was time to let it go, move on, and spend my effort on a client who wanted to hire my business and valued our pricing.

I probably put out more than 25 proposals in my first year of business; roughly 15 of them were not successful. Does it hurt? Yes, and with each experience I re-evaluate how I approached the client to see what I can do better in the future, but in the end if the client didn't hire me, there's nothing I can do for that client without being pushy. How many proposals you put work into compared to how many will actually work out will affect your financial bottom line, so be aware of your projected growth and potential for clients and know that a certain percentage of them will sign and the rest will not.

As you will see in the segmented pricing examples in section **3.**, it is completely okay to make changes and change your expectations of your business. That means each year you could and should increase your pricing based on your experience, exposure, and reputation.

Do not change your selected and structured price plan in the middle of the year; always do it at the start of the new year, and maintain that standard price structure until the end of that year.

I always recommend that you update your price structure at least a year prior to the changes coming into effect because clients will book you for that year coming up. In January 2014, I created a new pricing structure for January 2015.

From day one I've always said I would rather have 10 $5,000 weddings than 100 $500 weddings. It is not fair to myself, my staff, or my clients if I exhaust myself. Don't worry, you will find your comfort level and what your capabilities are, and what you feel you can handle may change every year.

Although you should stick to your pricing, be sure to always ask your client what his or her budget is. If it is a client that was looking forward to working with you, be sure to be negotiable and if possible, work within his or her budget. If it is far beyond what you know you are worth, though, then you may have to cut your losses. The point of setting up a fee structure is to maintain and grow the integrity of your business; if clients consistently are given a discount, they may question why you have your prices set so high in the first place.

The added bonus of being referred is that you know your vendors are providing you with potential clients who fit within your price structure. This generally will happen after working with that vendor a few times so they are aware and experienced with what your value is bringing to an event.

If a client expresses a need for a discount or tries to tell you that another planner provided him or her with a lower quote, you may feel obligated to offer a slight discount such as a "friends and family discount." However, you don't have to give the client a discount.

If he or she is still trying to negotiate with you after that, the project may not be the best fit for your business and you should walk away.

3. Levels of Event Planning Pricing

Setting a price point for your services can be dependent on your experience, exposure, and expectations. As your business grows you will be able to increase pricing. This is a sample breakdown of what to expect from service fees you provide.

The following sections are the three levels you need to consider, as you will want your company to fit one of them.

3.1 Affordable

Affordable means you will set your prices below competitive pricing in your area to increase the number of events you can produce. With this model, minimal marketing and promotion is needed as what sells your service is price. This model usually works best for a larger company with multiple employees, or a company with the ability to bid for freelance consultants. Lower cost will lead to an increase in the number of booked events. I recommend this model for businesses starting out for their first one to three years as a way to expose their company to clients, the local event industry, and other local vendors.

Another way to look at the numbers:

52 weekends

2 consultants = 2 weddings a weekend potential

104 possible events

$2,000 per event

$2,000 x 104 = $208,000 potential income for the company

$104,000 potential income per planner

$5,000 out-of-pocket expenses

$99,000 potential income for each planner

3.2 Noticed

Noticed means you actively participate in marketing promotions and advertising as well as offer services at the average price of a planner in your area. By creating promotional pieces such as rack cards and attending bridal shows, clients will be booking you based on what they see and whether they like it in the moment. Whether it be a magazine ad, online marketing, social media, or your website, any form of visual reference will be what sells your services. This model often works for seasoned professionals with experience and established connections with vendors. With this model, since you are portraying your esthetic, it is important to consider what reputation you wish to have among your colleagues. Find a niche that does not exist yet and be a master at it.

An individual planner or a partnership can benefit most from this model. This could be utilized by a company anywhere from year two to five of the business.

Another way to look at the numbers:

52 weekends

1 consultant = 1 wedding a weekend potential

52 possible events

$3,500 per event

$3,500 x 52 = $182,000 potential income per planner

$15,000 out-of-pocket expenses

$167,000 potential income for each planner

3.3 Referred

Referred is the most sought-after form of client booking. It means people are seeking YOUR company because they love the work you do or have heard rave reviews about your service, so you do not have to expend extreme effort in seeking clients. It allows for you to be selective in the type of clients you book since their desire to have an event planned by your company outweighs the cost. With this model, your business will flourish based on word of mouth from former clients as well as esteemed colleagues. Most of your expenses will go to maintaining relationships with these raving fans with lunch, holiday gifts, and other kinds of image maintenance. Your goal should be to reach this level by year five of your business.

Another way to look at the numbers:

52 weekends

1 consultant = 1 wedding a weekend potential

52 possible events

$5,000 per event

$5,000 x 52 = $260,000 potential income per planner

$20,000 out-of-pocket expenses

$240,000 potential income for each planner

That isn't to say that pricing is not negotiable as with most service providers. If there is a potential client, there's always room for negotiation but it should be based on your goals, financial stability, and prospects from doing a certain event.

A word about commissions: A planner will always refer you to the best available service providers, right? Not necessarily. Let's look at what motivates a planner to make referrals.

The most ethical planners will base their referrals on a client's goals and budget, suggesting the pros who will best meet the client's needs within those parameters. Is the entertainment what's most important because you want everyone to have a great time? This planner will find you the best options. Are you more of a foodie than a dancer? In this scenario the planner will help you allocate a larger portion of the budget to catering, and make suggestions accordingly. Giving you the very best experience possible is what's most important.

Other planners (and some venues, too), are more interested in maximizing their profit margins. They will only refer entities who pay them a percentage, or kickback for the referral. While this may be a valid business plan, the client then has to wonder if [he or she is] truly being introduced to the best possible services. Is the planner suggesting this band because [it is] genuinely the best band available within my budget? Or [is it] a mediocre band who gets the referral because they're lining the planner's pockets?

Three ways to assess a planner's approach on this subject:

1. Ask the planner directly what [his or her] philosophy is on the matter.

2. If you're contracting all of the services directly through the planner, ask to see the agreements between the planner and the service providers (this will be very telling).

3. Ask every photographer, DJ, and other service provider you speak to what planner they love to work with and why?

— Cindy Ormond, Owner, Ormond Entertainment

Charge appropriately! Your time and professional opinion is worth money. Do not undercharge for your services, or you will never make a living out of it.

— Alicia Graser,
Sales & Marketing Manager,
William's Florist & Gift House

4. Event Budgeting

It is crucial that you have a set event planning template for the client's budget. I currently have templates for a wedding planning budget, a day of coordination budget, a full event planning budget, a destination event budget, and a nonprofit event budget. If you create these templates early on in your business plan the ability to adjust and mimic them throughout each event is much easier, saving you time and money in the long run.

I have created a budget template that is all-inclusive for my clients. I have found throughout my career that many people who provide budgets will not include or eliminate specific costs so that they seem like they are creating an event within the client's budget.

Think of everything. Include taxes, gifts, travel, accommodations, and think outside the actual event itself and what costs of the clients will be incurred during the entire planning process and on the event execution day.

Many budgets forget to include the 20 percent administration fee and 8 percent tax (in New York State) to their budget for food and beverages. If the event were a $10,000 event then 20 percent of the food could quickly be one fifth of the overall budget. If you're not honest with the clients and provide them up front with knowledge of these additional fees, you are at fault. It is your job to manage, streamline, and educate your clients in all aspects of the event that they may not know. Let's face it, most of them are doing this event for the first time and if they're hiring an event planner, it's because they don't want to think about the small details that would potentially pop up or surprise them.

Do your job and provide the clients with knowledge of all possible financial burdens. This will build a level of trust and position you as an expert so clients will continue to want to work with you for future events.

Once I make my template for the event, I create a Google document with it and share it with the client. This allows us both to make changes and alterations to the original budget so we can see where the event is going and how finances can be distributed. I'm always sure to make a PDF file of the original budget so we can compare where we ended up to where we started. This is important for the growth of your business. You'll get to see how good you are at allocating costs and whether your ability to project budget and finances is fair to the client.

I always tell my clients it is my job to make their budgets work. I know the specific items at an event that are worth spending the money on, and those that aren't. Based on my experience guests don't notice. What is worth the additional dollars? It is your job as the event planner to guide and educate your clients on the choices they should make to have the best event possible.

Having a budget you can show clients explains exactly where the money is going and allows them to make the final choice to allocate to a different "I want."

They can then understand that if it is something they really want, it is going to cost a certain amount. One example is having live music at a ceremony; the average cost to have a quartet is currently about $500 in my area. Most people don't know this. If this is important to your clients, you need to put that into the budget and potentially maneuver money from somewhere else to accommodate the request (e.g., less expensive invitations).

In the end, always be honest with your clients, be open, and provide them with every single update of financial burden or cost they may incur. If a projected cost ends up being significantly higher than what you had allocated, be sure you inform the clients before you move forward and take action on that element. It is their money and you should be respectful of that.

An event budget will be part of every project and can be altered to the specific business, client, and event. A sample budget for a traditional wedding is shown in Sample 6. The budget template shown in Sample 7 is available in the download kit included with this book for your use. You can alter it to fit your business and any events you plan.

SAMPLE 6
PEAR SAMPLE BUDGET

PEAR SAMPLE	$40,000	200 guests	8 attendants	
NAME			Shannon Lach — Manager	
EVENT DATE	20-Sep-14		716.512.9166	
LAST UPDATED	4/15/14		shannon@pearplanning.com	
Description	**Qty**	**Unit Cost**	**Total Cost**	**Paid**
PERSONAL EFFECTS				
Marriage License	1	$40.00	$40.00	
Bride's Attire	1	$1,500.00	$1,500.00	
Wedding Accessories	1	$300.00	$300.00	
Groom's Attire	1	$200.00	$200.00	
Rings	0	$0.00	$0.00	
Attendant Gifts	8	$50.00	$400.00	
Hair	0	$150.00	$0.00	
Makeup: engagement	1	$60.00	$60.00	
Makeup: wedding	1	$100.00	$100.00	
SERVICE PROVIDER				
Wedding Planner	1	$5,000.00	$5,000.00	
Photographer	1	$4,000.00	$4,000.00	
Videographer	1	$3,000.00	$3,000.00	
Officiant			$0.00	
STATIONERY				
Save the Date	125	$1.75	$218.75	
Invitations	125	$5.00	$625.00	
Programs	75	$1.50	$112.50	
Escort Cards	125	$0.30	$37.50	
Menu Cards	200	$1.75	$350.00	
Table Numbers	0	$0.00	$0.00	
Tax		$0.09	$117.54	
Postage	250	$0.84	$210.00	
VENUE				
Ceremony Venue	1	$500.00	$500.00	
Reception Venue	1	$500.00	$500.00	
Cake Cutting	1	$0.00	$0.00	
TRANSPORTATION				
Bridal Couple/Party	1	$800.00	$800.00	
Wedding Guests	1	$0.00	$0.00	

MUSIC				
Ceremony	1	$300.00	$300.00	
Cocktails	1	$200.00	$200.00	
Reception	1	$2,000.00	$2,000.00	
Photo Booth	1	$800.00	$800.00	
FLORAL				
Personal	1	$800.00	$800.00	
Ceremony	1	$500.00	$500.00	
Reception	1	$2,000.00	$2,000.00	
DECOR RENTALS				
Ceremony	1	$200.00	$200.00	
Reception	1	$1,500.00	$1,500.00	
FOOD & BEVERAGE	Gluten Free/Vegetarian			
Meals	225	$24.95	$5,613.75	
Bar	200	$22.95	$4,590.00	
Wedding Cake	1	$500.00	$500.00	
Table Wine Service	0	$18.95	$0.00	
Tax		9%	$892.83	
Gratuity		18%	$1,836.68	
Specialty Drink			$0.00	
Appetizers	4	$150.00	$600.00	
OTHER EVENTS				
Rehearsal Dinner			$0.00	
Wedding Breakfast			$0.00	
Morning After Brunch			$0.00	
			$0.00	
MISC. ITEMS				
Favors	250	$1.00	$250.00	
Welcome Bags	0	$0.00	$0.00	
Wedding Items	0	$0.00	$0.00	
Overnight Accommodations	0	$0.00	$0.00	
			$40,654.55	

EVENT BUDGET WORKSHEET

Event Budget for [Event Name]

Expenses

Site	Estimated	Actual
Space Fee	$2,000.00	
Setup/Breakdown Fees	$1,000.00	
Clean up	$500.00	
Site Staff	$1,000.00	
Sound System		
Lighting System		
Staging		
Tables and Chairs		
Pipe & Drape		
Rental Linens		
Totals	$4,500.00	$0.00

Decorations	Estimated	Actual
Flowers		
Candles		
Banners/Signage		
Decor		
Supplies		
Totals	$0.00	$0.00

Publicity	Estimated	Actual
Graphic Design		
Photography/Video		
Printing		
Postage		
Advertising Print		
Advertising Online		
Webcasting		
Totals	$0.00	$0.00

Refreshments	Estimated	Actual
Food		
Drinks		
Corkage Fee		
Rental Linens		
Totals	$0.00	$0.00

Program/Entertainment	Estimated	Actual
Performers		
Speakers		
Travel		
Hotel		
Photographer		
Videographer		
Other		
Totals	$0.00	$0.00

Prizes	Estimated	Actual
Ribbons/Plaques/Trophies		
Gifts		
Totals	$0.00	$0.00

Miscellaneous	Estimated	Actual
Parking		
Security		
First Aid		
Liability Insurance		
Contingency		
Totals	$0.00	$0.00

Event Budget for [Event Name]

Expenses

	Estimated	Actual		Estimated	Actual
Communications			**Communications**		
Telephone					
Postage					
Stationery Supplies					
Wireless Connection					
Fax Services					
Totals	$0.00	$0.00	**Totals**	$0.00	$0.00
Permits					
Tent					
Liquor					
Parking					
Entertainment					
Other					
Totals	$0.00	$0.00	**Totals**	$0.00	$0.00
Totals	$0.00	$0.00	**Totals**	$0.00	$0.00

BUSINESS PAPERWORK, ACCOUNTING, AND INSURANCE

6

Now the not so fun part of owning a business that we all know about and want to avoid: Paperwork.

1. Business Names and Tax Numbers

Besides choosing the right name (as discussed earlier in this book), the most important paperwork you will need to do to start your business is to register a business name or DBA (doing business as). In the US, most businesses are required to obtain an Employer Identification Number (EIN) from the IRS and in Canada a Business Number (BN) from the CRA. These will be used by the IRS or CRA to track your taxes.

Obtain tax numbers for your area (information on how to do this and what is needed can also be obtained from the IRS and CRA).

The majority of event planners in smaller towns seem to just have a DBA in my experience, but I highly recommend if you are an independently opening a business or firm then you should register as a Limited Liability Company (LLC). This is important for many reasons, the main one being if someone were to sue you, the costs come directly out of the business not your personal life. It separates the responsibility of financial burden when a misfortune may

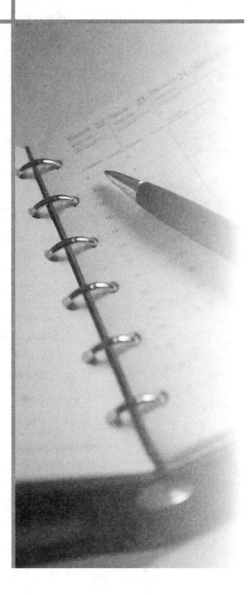

occur with your business and gives your life protection, now that people are no longer able to sue you because of something to do with your business and therefore take your car, house, or full bank account.

Getting your LLC can cost around $1,000 (in the US) so be sure to budget for this when you're planning your start-up budget. Be sure to consult with a business attorney in your area who is able to file the paperwork for you. I found my business attorney by attending local networking groups and getting referrals from friends.

It is okay for you to interview multiple lawyers because your lawyer is an important person who will be working closely with you throughout your entire business career. You need to enjoy communicating with this individual as well as trust him or her.

2. Business Licenses and Permits

Different provinces, states, and cities have different requirements for business licensing. A quick Google search, or phone call to City Hall in your area should get you some answers as to what you will need based on your specific circumstances.

3. Accountants and Bookkeepers

Find an accountant or a bookkeeper, especially if you are new to tracking the day-to-day expenses and income of a business, or doing business taxes. Ask your friends and colleagues who they would refer based on your need for accounting and bookkeeping.

A good accountant should take your receipts and organize them in a spreadsheet or similar way, for you to easily read and comprehend. He or she will help you allocate costs and file business taxes.

Trained accountants know where to look and can suggest ways to improve your business. The first year I was in business I did this work myself, and then I realized as business increased and finances increased I needed someone else to tell me what my options were.

3.1 Writing off items

I follow the practice of keeping every receipt that is in tune with my business. It is my accountant's job to separate and delegate where those finances go as well as educate me if something cannot be written off as a business expense.

If something is specifically bought for a client's event, it is important that you allocate that by writing the event name on the top of the receipt for your accountant.

Receipts to keep:

- Food, beverages (when working/entertaining clients).

- Gas.

- Office supplies.

- Furniture.

- Event items.

- Marketing and website costs.

- Rent, phone, and utilities.

- Tolls.

- Travel expenses and hotel stays.

Depending on your preference, when it comes to your car, you can either register it as a business vehicle or use it as a personal car and write off your mileage. Consistently track your mileage; this way you do not have to keep all of your gas receipts and it accounts for wear and tear on your car.

You can keep all of your gas receipts so that you can track the gas used for each individual event. I do both because even if my accountant does not need the gas receipts it helps me learn where my fee is going and how much I'm spending on specific events, which in turn will eventually lead to a better fee structure if needed.

Something that helps me keep my finances tracked is an Expense Reimbursement Sheet as shown in Sample 8. If you are diligent about filling out this type of form, and having employees do so as well, and keeping the forms and receipts in an orderly file, you will make your life (and your bookkeeper's or accountant's life) that much easier.

3.2 Daily paperwork

Perhaps you haven't yet found the right accountant or bookkeeper, or only want to pay one for major things, such as business taxes.

SAMPLE 8
EXPENSE REIMBURSEMENT

Your Company Name   **Expense Reimbursement Request**

Event Name

_____

Payee Name   *Expense Period Start Date*

_____

Payee Address

_____

City   *State*   *Zip*   *Expense Period End Date*

_____

Payee Signature   *Date*

Business Purpose for Expenses

Item	Expense Description	Amount
Mileage	From Buffalo NY – 144 Overlook Utica	$223.44
Purchase	tape, screwdriver, notebook	
	gas for Shannon's car	
Meals		
Office Supplies		
	Receipt or proof of items required	
	Total Amount:	$223.44

Office Use Only

Received by: **Reimbursement Approved:**   ☐ Yes

_____   ☐ No
Name

_____
Signature   *Date*

The day-to-day financial record-keeping is probably going to fall on you as the owner/operator of the business, at least in the beginning or until you get a business or an employee relationship set up with an accountant or a bookkeeper.

Some of the things you will need to keep an eye on are where the money is coming from (perhaps you will call this Accounts Receivable), and where it is going (Accounts Payable, or Expenses).

For accounts receivable, when it is time to bill a client, you'll want to provide him or her with an invoice (don't forget to charge the appropriate taxes for your area, which you hopefully have remembered to let your client know about when you quoted). You can create one from a free template you find in an office suite or online, add your logo, and alter to suit your needs. I use one that is kind of a running invoice, such as what is shown in Sample 9; it looks like an account statement, and is updated frequently as some projects and clients pay in instalments (all depending on the individual agreements, of course).

When you invoice a client, you'll keep a record of when you billed and what was paid when in a ledger such as what is shown in the Income Ledger in Sample 10.

When you spend money for the business you will also keep records in an Expense Ledger. See Sample 11.

Your invoices, ledgers, and expense reimbursement statements can be kept until tax season, at which time your accountant or bookkeeper will thank you for keeping everything in such good order.

4. Insurance

An oft-forgotten but most important thing to consider when starting a business is insurance. Talk to an insurance agent in your area about what insurance would be good for your business. You will want to think about having liability insurance, insurance for your location, office contents, and vehicle. Ask the agent if there is anything you are forgetting to insure.

PEAR
PLANNING EVENTS AND RECEPTIONS

NAME	Jane McMay		Shannon Lach — Manager	
EVENT DATE	20-Sep-14		555.555.5555	
LAST UPDATED	25-May-14		shannon@pearplanning.com	
DATE	BALANCE	PAYMENT	TYPE	PAID
10.25.12	$4,250.00	$60.00	cash	Y
11.21.12	$4,190.00	$480.00	cash	Y
2.28.13	$3,710.00	$2,000.00	cash	Y
09.09.13	$1,710.00	$1,000.00	check	Y
12.31.13	$710.00			
	$710.00			
	TOTAL PAID	$3,540.00		

SAMPLE 10
INCOME LEDGER

Invoice	Name	Date	Due Date	Amount	Total Paid	Date Paid	Owing
100	Jane McMay	Friday, June 13, 2014	Saturday, June 14, 2014	$ 2,000.00	$ 2,000.00	2/1/2009	$ -
101	John Winger	Sunday, June 15, 2014	Monday, June 16, 2014	$ 1,500.00	$ 1,500.00	4/10/2009	$ -
102	Ray Wong	Monday, June 16, 201.	Tuesday, June 17, 2014	$ 3,500.00		3/17/2009	$ 3,500.00
				$	$		$ -
							$ -
							$ -
							$ -
							$ -
							$ -
							$ -
Total				$ 7,000.00	$ 3,500.00		$ 3,500.00

Date	Store or Company	Invoice or Bill No.	Payment type	Amount		Total Paid		Date Paid	Outstanding	
Sunday, June 15, 2014	Walmart	n/a	cash	$	4.95	$	4.95		$	-
Sunday, June 15, 2014	Super Phone Company	12559	credit card	$	45.60	$	45.60		$	-
									$	-
									$	-
									$	-
									$	-
									$	-
									$	-
									$	-
									$	-
									$	-
									$	-
Total				$	50.55	$	50.55		$	-

PROMOTING AND MARKETING YOUR BUSINESS

7

Your business needs clients, and in order to get clients, you need to figure out how best to market and promote to your clientele.

1. Promoting Your Business

The number one rule to starting and continuing a successful business is networking; keep people in your loop to provide services that are best for you. I've always said that if I could, all of my friends who are vendors in the industry would get free services because I know that it is they who tell people about me, and essentially get me clients.

When I moved to Buffalo, New York, the first thing I learned about the event industry was that it's not that anyone will say anything good about you, rather that you're lucky if nobody says anything bad.

I am a firm believer in the best business is done over beer, not talking about business at all. You should get to know somebody before you decide you want to do business with him or her. It is about building relationships and connecting with people who can provide the same high-quality service that you expect of your business as well.

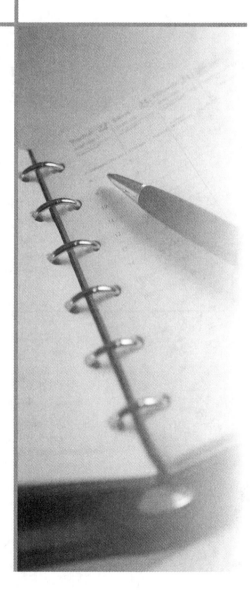

If done correctly, you will have free marketing and word-of-mouth advertising from these individuals as you uphold your part in promoting them as well.

Our PEARstyle editorial shoots have been crucial to the success of our business because they allow us to reach out to other businesses, new and distant, to partner with them and have them promoted throughout our company. PEARstyle editorial shoots are a collaboration of hand-selected vendors and service providers in the event industry that come together for a day of styling and faux event execution. Each participant, such as a florist, salon, and bakery, is given photographic rights to the images taken and they are put into our preferred vendor list. We also continuously market and support those who participate. Creating a community of event professionals benefiting from working together creates professional marketing material for all professionals involved, to have for website development and portfolio examples. It creates a community that continually supports all members.

In a sense it is a form of marketing our business has taken on. We do promotions and market the other businesses to show our appreciation for what they did to participate in our PEARstyle shoots.

In the same breath, the PEARstyle shoots are about having direct connection with preferred vendors and have them speak our praises. Because, let's face it, if it comes down to recommending a vendor, it is more likely you will recommend somebody you like, rather than just somebody else who is in the same industry.

1.1 Marketing etiquette

Marketing your business at your events is a delicate situation. I have always followed the rule that when clients hire me, I become an extension of them; company or couple. I have a standard policy that we do not promote our company, PEAR, at any social event. Although I have created an alternative to this challenge of not marketing PEAR at events: Each client has a golden pear placed somewhere at their event so guests and the client can recognize it. It could be placed at the escort table of a wedding, on a mantel at an anniversary dinner, or at a beverage station at a corporate holiday party. The key is modesty. Don't gloat, but be proud. I came up with this idea by thinking of high-end purses. When women see another woman holding the newest Louis Vuitton bag, they automatically associate confidence and status with that individual.

You don't pay $4,000 for a purse because it looks pretty, you buy it because it establishes status. You want to show your friends you can afford it and you appreciate the finer things in life.

I want that for my clients. I want them to be proud to be PEAR clients, and the small token of a pear at the event informs the guests they hired PEAR because they wanted the best event. Hopefully, in return, if the guests enjoy themselves, they will also want a golden PEAR at their event!

Corporate and nonprofit events lend more options to the possible promotion of your company, such as "event sponsorship" or "event produced by" with an opportunity to showcase your logo. Brochures, tickets, and invitations are other possible ways to promote your company within someone's event. Also, always carry dozens of business cards. Why would you not bring business cards to your job? It would be like a car dealer meeting you at the party, and selling you a car, then telling you he does not have any cards, but here is his website, and if you click in the right-hand corner, where it says "locations," you enter zip code 13499 and then search for Dave.

What? No. Who has time for that? Minimal effort for the client equals a greater return for your business.

You are allowed to hand out cards to guests, if they inquire about your services, but with discretion, and approval from the client.

Be cautious and be sure any presentation of your company name and logo is approved by the client! Angry clients do not make for good marketing, which would defeat the purpose.

The fact that your company is subtly prominent at the event will also narrow any gap you have to make mistakes; since everyone knows who produced it, you are held accountable!

2. The Marketing Pieces

Beyond a business card, you should always use three specific marketing pieces to promote your business. This rule of three is that you should never do any sort of marketing unless you can do it in three locations. The old standard was print, radio, and TV. Now we have technology and the increase in social media as a marketing platform, so it is easy to market your business in three places at the same time.

For new businesses I always recommend a website, Facebook business page, and a physical flyer as start-up marketing tools. In addition to your business card these marketing tools will allow you to reach and communicate with your clients as well as provide an inside look as to what your business does. Clients can also experience a day in the life of your business instantaneously if you post bits and pieces to your Facebook page.

2.1 Business card

Don't forget your business card, the first and simplest way to start marketing yourself. A simple tool to help you know what items you need to set up for your business is to think about your business card.

- Your name.
- Company name.
- Logo.
- Address.
- Email.
- Phone.
- Website URL.

All of these items should be in place before you launch your business.

Be sure to connect with a great graphic designer who can help you build your logo. Be aware that your logo and your company name are two completely different things. Our logo is a pear but our company name is PEAR as in "Planning Events and Receptions." You should always have a logo to coincide with your company name for easy recognition. (Think NIKE, Apple, Under Armour.)

2.2 Website

Building my website was the first thing I did after I registered my business name. I made sure the website I wanted was available and that it was descriptive about what I do. Our business name is PEAR, but unfortunately pear.com was taken. You need to be proactive about any URLs you want.

From there I started to look at my business from the standpoint of a client. If I were to give my website address to somebody and tell him or her my website was PearPlanning.com, he or she would automatically understand what we do: We plan. Though there are still questions about what PEAR means, that is okay, because the planning part also explains our business.

The website should be a location on the Web where individuals can see pictures or portfolios and get information. A lot of businesses, including my own, have started doing a continuous blog on the main page of their sites. I have found success in this because every time I post something new it draws in the clients. From there, if they have more questions, they can look directly on the website, rather than having to go to another site. Unless your business and structure requires otherwise, I recommend having a blog as part of your site to get people interested in hiring you.

Always make sure your email address is @yourbusinesswebsite.com. It is viewed as unprofessional to have a Gmail account or Yahoo! account as your email address for your business.

If you have an office location or storefront, it is best to get a landline for your business. If you're unable to start your business with a landline, I suggest you get a second cell phone number that can be used for your business only. Do not use your personal number as your business number. You should also work toward eventually having an office location or storefront, and your secretary or executive assistant will be using that phone number to sift through phone calls and run the office while you are on vacation. Dreams come true, right? Remember to think big and think over-the-top. You can do this, all you need to do is set your mind to it.

2.3 Social media

When utilizing Facebook, be aware there is a personal page and a business page option. It is bad business practice to make your personal page a business page. By all means, you can share what your business is doing on your personal page but all business information should be directly on a business page. This is common practice and shows respect for your friends, because a business page is where people have to opt in to follow what you're saying.

Utilizing Facebook as a marketing tool helps keep information fresh and lets you communicate intimately with your clients. It allows you to post every day or multiple times a day, to increase your fan base. It is also a great platform for interaction. You want to interact with clients as well as have them interact with you. Gauge what your fans want to see by analyzing the statistics Facebook gives you. This piece of marketing is more fun, it allows you to show personality in your business as well as connect with other colleagues and event vendors. Be sure to always be appropriate, kind, and professional on your Facebook page because it is a marketing tool that anyone can access. Be sure never to badmouth a client, vendor, or professional in public because that will harm your reputation!

Facebook is a good place to express your individual ideas and thoughts about a certain situation as well as the creative reflection of ideas. If you firmly believe in something controversial, I recommend you reserve it for your personal page rather than your business page.

Other social media sites such as Instagram, Foursquare, Twitter, and Pinterest are also used by companies to showcase their thoughts, brag about achievements, or (in the case of Pinterest) post ("pin") images to get people thinking about their events.

2.4 Flyers, pamphlets, rack cards, and brochures

I think it is also important to have a physical flyer so that individuals can notice your business in physical locations (i.e., not just online). Be sure the design, word choice, and colors on this flyer reflect exactly what your business practices are about. The aesthetics you present on these marketing tools will draw in a certain type of client.

Do you like bold colors such as hot pink, lime green, and purple, or are you more of a subdued business owner who uses monochromatic schemes? Be aware that the potential client base resonates with color choices as well as font choices. To find out more about this, research at your local library for marketing tools and guidance, or consult a trained graphic designer to help you build your marketing pieces.

If you partner with another business, their opinion on color and design will likely matter too. See Sample 12 for an example of a flyer/rack card I have used a variation of in the past.

Physical marketing tools can include a service pamphlet, such as the example we use in Sample 13: A service pamphlet featuring weddings by PEAR.

3. Other Ways to Promote Yourself

There are other ways you can promote yourself. Be creative!

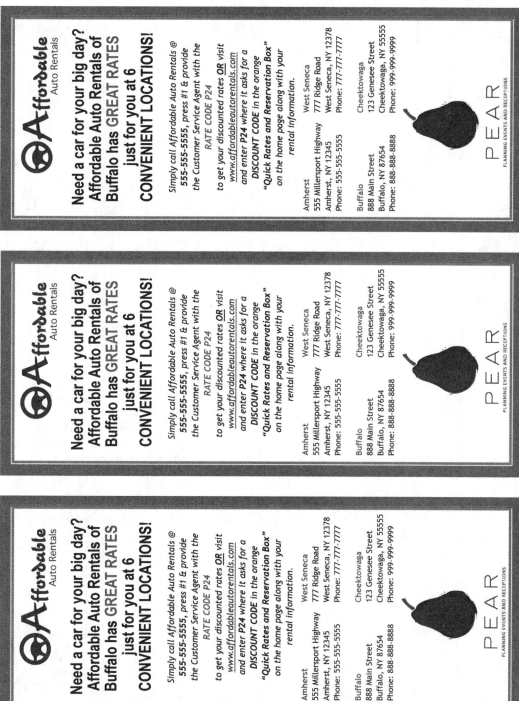

⊘Affordable
Auto Rentals

Need a car for your big day?
Affordable Auto Rentals of
Buffalo has GREAT RATES
just for you at 6
CONVENIENT LOCATIONS!

Simply call Affordable Auto Rentals @
***555-555-5555**, press #1 & provide*
the Customer Service Agent with the
RATE CODE P24
*to get your discounted rates **OR** visit*
www.affordableautorentals.com
*and enter **P24** where it asks for a*
***DISCOUNT CODE** in the orange*
*"**Quick Rates and Reservation Box**"*
on the home page along with your
rental information.

Amherst
555 Millersport Highway
Amherst, NY 12345
Phone: 555-555-5555

West Seneca
777 Ridge Road
West Seneca, NY 12378
Phone: *777-777-7777*

Buffalo
888 Main Street
Buffalo, NY 87654
Phone: 888-888-8888

Cheektowaga
123 Genesee Street
Cheektowaga, NY 55555
Phone: 999-999-9999

P E A R
PLANNING EVENTS AND RECEPTIONS

Affordable
Auto Rentals

Hitch a Ride with Affordable Auto Rentals of Buffalo

Wedding Transportation Tips:

Don't get stranded at the ceremony — follow these transportation tips and you'll be riding in style:

- **Know your options.** Sure there's always a stretch limo to ride in, but there are plenty of other choices when it comes to transportation. There's the standard town car, an SUV, Ford Crown Victoria — and those are just a few choices for automobiles.

- **Who's going?** Do you need to provide transportation for all the guests, just the bridal party, or solely the bride and groom? Naturally that will dictate which options are realistic for you. It's a nice touch to offer transportation for out-of-town guests who might not have a car available.

- **Work out the budget.** For the standard limo, expect to pay about $45-$60 per hour, plus gratuity, which is anywhere from 15% to 20%. For a typical five-hour wedding, that's about $250-$360. Be sure to check the bill for automatic gratuity before you add in that extra money. Those prices are just for standard limos, and don't include any upgrades like a sunroof or champagne.

- **Speaking of champagne...** You can request extras such as champagne from the car company. If you choose to not go that route, buy your own before the wedding and stash it in the vehicle. After the ceremony, you and your new spouse can have your first toast as a wedding couple in the privacy of your own automobile.

- **Scale back.** To keep transportation costs manageable, consider only getting a car for the newly wedded couple. A car that seats two will be much less expensive than one for 20. The bridal party can carpool to the reception site.

- **Time it right.** This is more about planning correctly than transportation, but you should be aware of the route to get to the reception and how long it takes. (Get in the car and drive it yourself, if possible, going at the same time and day of the week as your wedding will be.) If your ceremony ends at 4:30 p.m. and the reception begins at 5:30 p.m. but it only takes 20 minutes to head over, what will your guests do with that extra 40 minutes? Standing around outside the reception site gets boring after about 10 minutes.

- **Anticipate parking problems.** This is especially pertinent if you're getting married in a city that's notorious for problematic parking. The first rule of thumb is that your guests shouldn't have to pay extra to attend your wedding. If possible, attempt to find free parking in the area (let guests know in advance if there will be a distance to walk) or figure out a way to validate parking vouchers. You might also consider using a valet service (about $20-$25 per hour per attendant), which can cut down on parking problems. Non-valet attendants can also be helpful in directing traffic and answering parking questions.

Affordable
Auto Rentals

Hitch a Ride with Affordable Auto Rentals of Buffalo

Wedding Transportation Tips:

Don't get stranded at the ceremony — follow these transportation tips and you'll be riding in style:

- **Know your options.** Sure there's always a stretch limo to ride in, but there are plenty of other choices when it comes to transportation. There's the standard town car, an SUV, Ford Crown Victoria — and those are just a few choices for automobiles.

- **Who's going?** Do you need to provide transportation for all the guests, just the bridal party, or solely the bride and groom? Naturally that will dictate which options are realistic for you. It's a nice touch to offer transportation for out-of-town guests who might not have a car available.

- **Work out the budget.** For the standard limo, expect to pay about $45-$60 per hour, plus gratuity, which is anywhere from 15% to 20%. For a typical five-hour wedding, that's about $250-$360. Be sure to check the bill for automatic gratuity before you add in that extra money. Those prices are just for standard limos, and don't include any upgrades like a sunroof or champagne.

- **Speaking of champagne...** You can request extras such as champagne from the car company. If you choose to not go that route, buy your own before the wedding and stash it in the vehicle. After the ceremony, you and your new spouse can have your first toast as a wedding couple in the privacy of your own automobile.

- **Scale back.** To keep transportation costs manageable, consider only getting a car for the newly wedded couple. A car that seats two will be much less expensive than one for 20. The bridal party can carpool to the reception site.

- **Time it right.** This is more about planning correctly than transportation, but you should be aware of the route to get to the reception and how long it takes. (Get in the car and drive it yourself, if possible, going at the same time and day of the week as your wedding will be.) If your ceremony ends at 4:30 p.m. and the reception begins at 5:30 p.m. but it only takes 20 minutes to head over, what will your guests do with that extra 40 minutes? Standing around outside the reception site gets boring after about 10 minutes.

- **Anticipate parking problems.** This is especially pertinent if you're getting married in a city that's notorious for problematic parking. The first rule of thumb is that your guests shouldn't have to pay extra to attend your wedding. If possible, attempt to find free parking in the area (let guests know in advance if there will be a distance to walk) or figure out a way to validate parking vouchers. You might also consider using a valet service (about $20-$25 per hour per attendant), which can cut down on parking problems. Non-valet attendants can also be helpful in directing traffic and answering parking questions.

Affordable
Auto Rentals

Hitch a Ride with Affordable Auto Rentals of Buffalo

Wedding Transportation Tips:

Don't get stranded at the ceremony — follow these transportation tips and you'll be riding in style:

- **Know your options.** Sure there's always a stretch limo to ride in, but there are plenty of other choices when it comes to transportation. There's the standard town car, an SUV, Ford Crown Victoria — and those are just a few choices for automobiles.

- **Who's going?** Do you need to provide transportation for all the guests, just the bridal party, or solely the bride and groom? Naturally that will dictate which options are realistic for you. It's a nice touch to offer transportation for out-of-town guests who might not have a car available.

- **Work out the budget.** For the standard limo, expect to pay about $45-$60 per hour, plus gratuity, which is anywhere from 15% to 20%. For a typical five-hour wedding, that's about $250-$360. Be sure to check the bill for automatic gratuity before you add in that extra money. Those prices are just for standard limos, and don't include any upgrades like a sunroof or champagne.

- **Speaking of champagne...** You can request extras such as champagne from the car company. If you choose to not go that route, buy your own before the wedding and stash it in the vehicle. After the ceremony, you and your new spouse can have your first toast as a wedding couple in the privacy of your own automobile.

- **Scale back.** To keep transportation costs manageable, consider only getting a car for the newly wedded couple. A car that seats two will be much less expensive than one for 20. The bridal party can carpool to the reception site.

- **Time it right.** This is more about planning correctly than transportation, but you should be aware of the route to get to the reception and how long it takes. (Get in the car and drive it yourself, if possible, going at the same time and day of the week as your wedding will be.) If your ceremony ends at 4:30 p.m. and the reception begins at 5:30 p.m. but it only takes 20 minutes to head over, what will your guests do with that extra 40 minutes? Standing around outside the reception site gets boring after about 10 minutes.

- **Anticipate parking problems.** This is especially pertinent if you're getting married in a city that's notorious for problematic parking. The first rule of thumb is that your guests shouldn't have to pay extra to attend your wedding. If possible, attempt to find free parking in the area (let guests know in advance if there will be a distance to walk) or figure out a way to validate parking vouchers. You might also consider using a valet service (about $20-$25 per hour per attendant), which can cut down on parking problems. Non-valet attendants can also be helpful in directing traffic and answering parking questions.

PEAR SERVICE PAMPHLETS (Weddings by PEAR)

WEDDINGS

by
P E A R

PLANNING EVENTS AND RECEPTIONS

Love me, the way I love you...I do.

www.pearplanning.com

Shannon@pearplanning.com

PO Box 511

Buffalo, New York 14240

716 + 512 + 9166

Day of Planning {$2,000}

♥ Unlimited Planner Contact via Phone and Email
♥ Unlimited Time Day of Wedding
♥ Attendance at Rehearsal
♥ Vendor Liaison & Coordination
♥ Event Timeline Creation
♥ Review of All Contracts
♥ Two Meetings with Planner
♥ Trademark PEAR Gift
♥ Peace of Mind Day of Wedding

We expect the best,
We are the best...

Love
IYOU

Full Planning {$5,000}

♥ Full Preliminary Budget
♥ Recommended Vendors
♥ Planning Outline
♥ Unlimited Client Meetings
♥ Unlimited Vendor Meetings
♥ Unlimited Advice and Ideas
♥ Storage of Wedding Items
♥ Customized Design Concepts
♥ Includes All Day of Services

3.1 Join local organizations

Join a networking group or public speaking group to get to know people within and outside of the industry, such as a local chapter for the Chamber of Commerce, or any other industry leading organizations. See Chapter 8 for more about networking.

3.2 Practice an elevator speech

Having a successful elevator speech is also important, as sometimes you will only have 30 seconds to make an impression and sell your services. Hopefully you think this through as you are creating your business plan, as discussed in Chapter 4.

Here are a few taglines and elevator speeches we use at PEAR:

- Pear: Like the fruit.

- We are a western New York elite event management firm specializing in weddings, private social events, and holiday parties.

- Not only do we manage your time, we manage your budget; our skills lay in more than 11 years of experience manipulating numbers and dissecting contracts and pricing to get you the dream event without sacrificing your wallet or vision.

- PEAR: The most influential event planner in Upstate New York.

- Life is a series of events, let PEAR help you plan them.

- We look forward to "PEARing" up with you on the event.

3.3 Get some free publicity

The most effective kind of free publicity is being interviewed and published in blogspots, articles, or reviews. Anytime you have the opportunity to do an interview or offer a suggestion for an article, do it. Reach out to your local colleges and Chamber of Commerce to ask if you can present at their meetings to educate individuals on the purpose of your business. This way your name and business will be printed in the agenda ahead of time for people to research what you do. Brand recognition!

Though this type of exposure is at the cost of your personal time it is well worth the investment and effort. Point in fact, if I did not follow these suggestions, I would not be writing this book. Again think long-term, think big, and run for those goals.

NETWORKING

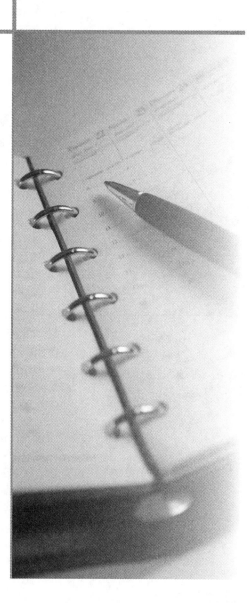

8

I am not shy about the one reason my business has been continuously growing and has succeeded in such a short time, is networking. I once was at an event for a local college and I was approached by an individual asking, "Are you Shannon from PEAR?," to which I replied "Yes." She then told me that a friend of a friend told her at a party that since she was planning her wedding, if she wanted the best event planner, she had to hire PEAR.

Event planning is a service-based industry. We gain and retain our business based on our service and event execution. Other than the execution of the final event, there is nothing physical that we can show people that proves we're good at what we do. There is no instantaneous or immediate reference to our work, other than the kind words of others.

For example, a photographer has a photo album for a portfolio, a DJ has music soundtracks, a florist has sample bouquets, but event planners are so personally involved in the planning process making each experience unique that it is often difficult for us to convey what we do other than by recommendations from others. That belief can be conveyed by our network of vendors and our colleagues who trust us, and let us show them that our best interest is always the client. We make it clear to individuals we will do whatever we can to make sure that the planning process for each client is seamless and stress free, so that they may refer us to clients in need of our help.

If you respect the industry as a whole, eventually the kindness and benefits will be yours as well.

Fifty percent of my business in year three was from word-of-mouth referrals from current clients. At every event I have anywhere between 5 to 15 individuals (based on an event of 150) approach me and ask me for my card because somebody they know is either getting married or they work for a business that throws an annual event. The "icing on the cake," so to speak, is having individuals approach you, who have asked the clients about their experience, and they say the first thing they should do is hire you as an event planner. That is effective networking at its finest.

When the other service providers and vendors see how grateful your client is and how impressed potential clients are at the event you're working, they will be more inclined to recommend you because you are experienced in the process of planning an event. I make the planning process as seamless as possible for the vendors involved. The last thing I want to do is to make their jobs harder.

I am humbled by the fact that I have become somewhat of a connection guru in the event industry, where individuals of other event businesses consistently contact me with questions and connections to others who may be appropriate for their clients' needs, such as a photographer, DJ, or florist.

Networking takes time; it is about sacrificing your time and pride and really doing research in the market to see who you want to connect with. We sometimes forget that getting to know someone is as simple as a phone call or an email. Most of my business connections started with either a Facebook message or an email letting them know I was interested in getting to know their business more. When you're networking, it is important to remember that the goal is not about selling yourself, it's about learning about them. Spend your time with them understanding who they are as individuals and as a company. From there you can assess if this company is in line with what you want to provide your clients. Oftentimes, individuals feel as though business networking is about small talk and money. This is not necessarily the case in a small industry when you're starting out.

Perhaps only once I have heard of a vendor recommending a service provider to a client because they were really good at what they did but the vendor felt that the person was an awful person and business owner. Everyone I interviewed and spoke with said they would rather refer clients to people they enjoyed as individuals as well as liked as colleagues.

Stay humble. I beg you to stay humble. As much as I am proud of my success in the event industry I always maintain a level of humility, especially when networking. You never know, one conversation with an individual may lead to multiple clients. For example, you are reading this book with intentions of learning something new about yourself and your business. Take each conversation and interaction with individuals the same exact way, and ask yourself "What can I learn from them?" What can you gain from this moment in time in which you get to speak with someone you have never before met?

To maintain a networking connection, you have to always be sure to follow up, and send contacts an email or a note saying you enjoyed meeting with them, and that you look forward to speaking with them again. Just try it, I bet you it will work.

When networking, it is important to remember one simple fact: Success in business is not about making people love you, it is about not giving them a reason to hate you. If no one is saying anything bad about you, you are being successful. Don't give them any reason to say something bad!

The best thing we can do is pay more attention to ourselves and allow others to be as they are. This is the easiest way to grow as a business owner.

An important part of business is to connect with vendors in your area that maintain the same standards that you do. Be open to participating in events with new vendors regardless of how many years you have been in service. The best event planner stays on top of trends and connects with new and upcoming talent. The way I have done this is to create PEARstyle editorial shoots, involving various vendors in the event planning industry to showcase their talent. It also allows me to spend quality time with them and work with them to see if their personality and way of executing work is something that is comparable and reasonable to the clients' expectations that I am booking.

Most of my marketing comes from supporting and promoting other businesses. I do this by exposing untapped, raw talent in the event industry who are not on the radar yet. Connecting with new individuals and providing the services creates a camaraderie and relationship between you and that business as well as makes you look as if you are innovative and the first to know new business, because you are showing something new and fresh before anybody else. You look as if you are on top of all the trends.

PEAR became a successful business within a year is partially because I connected with local businesses and they became my best marketing. Within six months I was told by a stranger that she was told by a local photographer I've never met that "if you want a wedding planner you have to hire PEAR because they are the best in the industry." Again, this was before I even had any clients.

My ability to network and research untapped, unexposed talent led to many national accounts and relationships where I could connect with event planning professionals and advertisers as a source for them to recruit new talent. It also built my recognition and reputation in the industry allowing me to post and be proud of the work I have done. This led me to multiple new clients.

They often say it's not what you do, it is who you know and unfortunately there is some truth to this statement. I believe that who you know gets you the meeting, and what you do gets you the job.

One of the major things I've learned so far is that making connections with other vendors is a must! Knowing who to go to for certain things makes our job that much easier! I've met and clicked with so many wonderful people in the industry! Event planning people are so much more fun than restaurant people!

— *Marie Kaminski,*
Event Manager, Magnolia Events

As a florist, working with a good planner versus a bad planner is like night and day, and it mostly comes down to budgeting. A good planner has trusted vendors. If a planner is taking a bride to four different florists, the bride might as well be doing it herself.

— *Alicia Graser,*
Sales & Marketing Manager,
Williams Florist & Gift house

1. Who to Connect With

I find it easiest to segment the groups of individuals with whom I want to network. This allows me to coordinate meetings, create possible introductions, and grow a sustainable contact list and invite list to upcoming PEAR events, based on their grouping.

The top three groups I recommend you segment your connections into are:

- Networking List: This is your practical list. For a wedding, it would include people and items such as DJ, florist, venue, photographer.

- Courage List: Who can you contact for a little extra exposure? Think business schools, local TV shows, radio.

- Ambitious List: Who would it be your dream to work for? Think government officials, or sports teams.

These groups have been the most influential in building my business. The list will also provide a seamless function to finding individuals in a specific field who may be contacted regarding a needed resource or inquiry for an event.

Keep your friends close, and keep your business connections closer!

I also suggest you create a list of connections you'd like to make, and think about including vendors and organizations as shown in Sample 14 (alter it to meet your needs; it is also available in the download kit).

Apparel: Bride

_____
_____
_____
_____

Apparel: Groom

_____
_____
_____
_____

Attorney

_____
_____
_____
_____

Business Networking Groups

_____
_____
_____
_____

Cake

_____
_____
_____
_____

Calligrapher

_____
_____
_____
_____

Caterer

_____
_____
_____
_____

Chamber of Commerce

_____
_____
_____
_____

Coffee Shop Owner

_____
_____
_____

College Internship Directors

_____
_____
_____

Colleges/Universities Course Directors

_____
_____
_____

Computer Person

_____
_____
_____

Convention Centers

_____
_____
_____
_____

Decor

_____

_____

_____

Favors

_____

_____

_____

Florist

_____

_____

_____

Franchise Owner (such as a Tim Hortons)

_____

_____

_____

Graphic Designer

_____

_____

_____

Hairstylist

_____

_____

_____

Hotel Sales Managers

_____

_____

_____

Liquor Stores

_____

_____

_____

Local Artists and Designers

_____
_____
_____

Local Bands

_____
_____
_____

Makeup Artist

_____
_____
_____

Music: Ceremony

_____
_____
_____

Music: Cocktails

_____
_____
_____

Music: Reception

_____
_____
_____

Networking Groups (BNI)

_____
_____
_____

News Reporter

_____
_____
_____

Newspaper Editor

_____

_____

_____

Officiant

_____

_____

_____

Overnight Accommodations

_____

_____

_____

Photo Booth

_____

_____

_____

Photographer

_____

_____

_____

Public Relations Manager

_____

_____

_____

Restaurant Owners

_____

_____

_____

Sign Designer

_____

_____

_____

Small Business Association (SBA) or Similar Organizations

_____
_____
_____

Stationery

_____
_____
_____

Tent and Rental Company

_____
_____
_____

Transportation

_____
_____
_____

Travel Agent

_____
_____
_____

Venue: Ceremony

_____
_____
_____

Venue: Reception

_____
_____
_____

Venue: Rehearsal

_____
_____
_____

Videographer

_____

_____

_____

Village Committees

_____

_____

_____

Wedding Planner

_____

_____

_____

Young Professionals' Groups

_____

_____

_____

WHY SOME EVENT PLANNERS ARE BETTER THAN OTHERS

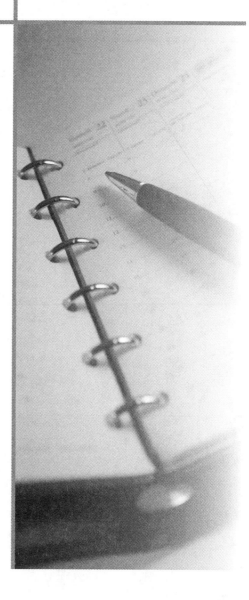

9

In this chapter I will discuss what makes some event planners better than others.

1. Why Some Event Planners Get Hired over Others

Hiring an event planner is like going out to eat for dinner. You could potentially make dinner yourself, but perhaps it is a special occasion and you want to enjoy the entire experience of the celebration.

Steak at home costs you $10, but $30 at a restaurant because you do not have to shop for it, prepare it, cook it, and serve it. Same with your drink. Bottle service at a club could be $300 and up because you are getting an experience and status among those who are in attendance since you paid the money to have an elite service.

It is the same with event planning for your clients. They can potentially do it themselves, but really, they should enjoy the process and the experience.

For this reason, there will always be a demand for event planners. People want to let someone else take care of the details so they can enjoy the experience.

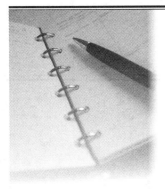

Communication: There will likely be many important individuals involved in the success of your wedding day ... think officiant, musicians, parents, bridesmaids, groomsmen, photographer(s), videographer(s), the band and/or DJ, catering staff, baker, florist, drivers ... to name a few! And there are often many different components and time frames involved, too. A great wedding planner will not only make sure everyone is informed in the days leading up to the wedding, but will also make sure everyone has up-to-the-minute info on the day of, too. Planners act as "central command" while you are enjoying each moment, worry free.

— *A local NY DJ*

2. Making Your Event Stand Out: Modern Tips

Here are some tips to make your modern event stand out:

- Guest interactive moments (e.g., magician).

- Standing cocktail versus seated dinner.

- Color choices versus black and white.

- Getting married? Wear a colored dress instead of white!

- Having a celebratory cake? Why not do a custom cake made of macaroons, Oreos, or doughnuts instead? The single serving options makes it more accessible for guests and the compensation still goes to the bakery!

- Present your food in modern ways, such as a mashed potato martini or a shot of soup.

- Have an "anti theme" by using a decade of time, or a color of the emphasized event element.

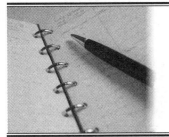

You want to enjoy your event! A planner will make things look better than you thought was even possible ... you're paying for [his or her] experienced eye.

— *Alicia Graser,*
Sales & Marketing Manager,
Williams Florist & Gift house

- Think outside the venue. Buildings are so over! Why not plan a bar mitzvah on a boat, or a corporate holiday party in an airplane hangar, rent out the local baseball field for a birthday party, or be center stage and plan a wedding in a theater?

- Imagine what you think you couldn't do somewhere, and do it!

3. Technological Advances in Event Planning

As mobile and portable communication devices begin to saturate the working world, it is an ever growing necessity to incorporate these into your business plans. A new sense of urgency and expectations of immediate responses have been instilled in us due to this increase in technology and it is imperative you allow yourself to explore using these technologies in your business. Tablets, laptops, GPS, and cell phones are a few items which have made my day-to-day business communications easier.

Concierge: Left your Manolo Blahniks at the house? Not sure how you'll transport the flower arrangements from the church to the reception? Groomsmen need help pinning their boutonnieres? Having trouble with your bustle? Realizing you started your day at 8:00 a.m., dinner is not until 7:00 p.m., and you need something more substantial than a Snickers bar to tide you over? Your wedding planner can do it all!

Clairvoyance: Odds are the marrying duo has never before planned a wedding from start to finish, and are completely unaware of all the variables that can influence the day. Meanwhile, a wedding planner often has years of experience to draw from, and will be able to anticipate and solve potential glitches before they even happen. How's that for peace of mind?

— *Cindy Ormond,* Owner, Ormond Entertainment

As I spend 80 percent of my time either in meetings, or on my way to meetings, having access to my clients and the ability to research is invaluable and saves me time and money in the long run.

Of course, we all know time is money. Especially in the event planning world! Make the most of your moments all while being aware enough to separate your professional life and personal life. Dedicate time specifically for both. Even with technology and portable communication, be sure everything you do is with full mindfulness and not in the absence of thought.

Do you struggle with your inner "DIY" self? A planner is experienced in knowing what is worth spending the money on to have someone else do, and what is worth putting together yourself, while keeping the budget in mind. Your time and your planner's time for DIY is worth money, too.

— *Alicia Graser,*
Sales & Marketing Manager,
Williams Florist & Gift house

4. Greening Your Event

Being mindful of ecological and environmental concerns is the best way to "green" your event. I am not saying everything has to be recycled or repurposed, and please don't try to illuminate a barn with only candles (although that would look stunning).

When trying to make an event more environmentally friendly, I think of the tradition and then create an alternative. Want a ceremony program and a dinner menu? Why not combine them on a double-sided flyer? Then have a basket labeled "programs" so guests can tastefully recycle the paper at the reception.

Balloons are also fun, but the latex can be hazardous to the environment, and really, where do they land? Hopefully not on your car in the middle of winter! Instead, look at the balloon upside-down: Instead of having floating balloons, have hanging pompons!

Try e-vites instead of paper invitations.

My favorite green decor element is plant seedlings instead of floral centerpieces. Small, blooming trees or plants placed in decorated planters can provide the same height and "awe" factor as a towering floral arragement. The best part of this is that my clients can share the seedlings with loved ones or a local not-for-profit that can plant them into the earth the following week. Nothing goes to waste and all comes full circle. I think that is the ultimate green goal, right?

From a Bride: Why You Should Hire an Event Planner

1. Time.

2. Stress.

3. You will not be "over" your wedding by the time it comes.

Reality is I work a ton of crazy hours and the free time I do have I want to spend with my family and friends or do something relaxing. Having a wedding planner lets you keep your free time, while still having the peace of mind that things are still being done.

Who doesn't stress over their wedding? Well I don't actually because I have a planner who takes care of anything and everything. My favorite line through my entire engagement has been "I don't know, ask my planner." The amount of questions (vendors/family/friends) ask you during the planning stage is incredibly overwhelming. Having a planner takes away all of that stress because you do not need to have any answers.

When you hire a planner, [her] passion is to plan weddings. That's why [she] became a wedding planner. It keeps your wedding day special and allows you to enjoy the planning process instead of being "over it" by the time it actually comes.

Another reason I enjoy having a wedding planner is [he or she is] always excited. I can call my planner and tell her I bought new shoes for my bridal shower and she is excited. It's the one person that will never tire talking about your wedding. She can figure out all of those crazy family traditions that need to happen the day of and intercept those obnoxious people you actually don't want to deal with.

— Emilee Okon,
PEAR Bride/Client

FORTUNE IS IN THE FOLLOW-UP

10

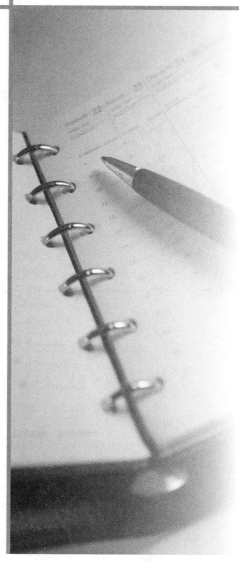

The most prosperous aspect of my business has been creating and implementing follow-up procedures. The ability to maintain a connection and stay in the forefront of potential clients' minds is priceless.

"Fortune is in the follow-up" goes for everything in terms of vendors as well as clients. When I meet with somebody I socially acknowledge him or her on Facebook or Twitter. After every single event, I send every vendor I connected with a thank-you card for his or her services. It is also very important to follow up with your clients, either it be a bride, a not-for-profit, or a corporate client. Be sure to send people a thank-you card within seven days of the event to show that you are proud to have been a part of it. This may help them remember to hire you for future events.

Follow up with those individuals again six to eight months after the event and send them a "thinking of you" card or find another way to keep in touch with them.

It wasn't until this year that I understood why businesses send out Christmas cards. This keeps people aware of you each year, increasing the possibility of referrals if they remember you.

You want to be the first thought on their minds when someone mentions "event planner," and following up with them can do this.

Other tactics I have used for maintaining close relationships within my network are as follows:

- 25 days of surprises: Out of our list of potential contacts, I pick 25 random names to send $5 coffee gift cards to with "have a happy day" notes and my business card.

- We hand out real pears at events and on our birthday to local shops and restaurants.

- We made beer coasters with our logo and website on them and hand them out to bars.

The thing to remember is make your follow-up genuine, sincere, and memorable!

I truly thank you for taking the time to read this book and trusting me as an advisor on your journey to creating your own event planning company. Even though these are some tools and tricks I have used in my own business, you don't have to follow them exactly. The trick is to always be confident in who you are and what you want your business to be. Reference and research how you want to form your business and be sure to be proud of what you're producing 100 percent. Being proud is a guaranteed way to be sure you create a business in which will be successful and that you can stand behind, knowing it is what you love.

I wish you the best of luck on your journey and I look forward to receiving your emails and letters! I hope even one part of this book helped you become a more confident event planner.

See you in the next book!

You can find me online:

ShannonLach@pearplanning.com

www.pearplanning.com

facebook.com/pearplanning

Or by mail:

PO Box 511
Buffalo, New York 14240

DOWNLOAD KIT

Please enter the URL you see in the box below into your computer web browser to access and download the kit.

www.self-counsel.com/updates/meetingevent/14kit.htm

The kit includes forms in PDF, MS Excel, and MS Word formats. You can print and edit some of the forms to meet your needs:

- Start-up Checklist
- Business Plan
- Phone Answering and Voicemail Rules
- Introductory Letter
- Destination Wedding Contract
- Start-up Costs Worksheet
- Expense Reimbursement
- Invoice
- Income Ledger
- Expense Ledger
- PEAR Rack Cards
- PEAR Service Pamphlets (Weddings by PEAR)
- Networking Connections
- Resources

OTHER TITLES OF INTEREST FROM SELF-COUNSEL PRESS

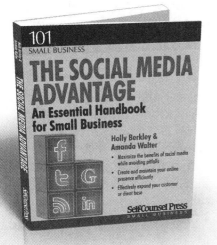

The Social Media Advantage

Holly Berkley and Amanda Walter
ISBN: 978-1-77040-142-6
8¼ x 9¾ • paper + CD-ROM • 176 pp.
First edition
$17.95 USD/CAD

In just a few short years, social media has become a world-wide phenomenon where Facebook updates or tweets can be mini press releases read by thousands of people every day. With this book your small business can get in the game, using social media as a free public relations tool!

Think of today's social media as customer service that transforms into virtual word-of-mouth marketing, which can have a huge impact, if done correctly. Some users may have hundreds of followers, so even a single mention of your business can immensely expand your visibility online!

The Authors

Holly Berkley is a website producer and Internet marketing consultant with more than 15 years of experience. Her Internet marketing company, Berkley Web Strategies, merged with a top hosting and technology company to form Vantage Internet Services. Holly is now an independent consultant. She is also the author of *Low-Budget Online Marketing for Small Business and Marketing in the New Media*.

Amanda Walter is a PR professional who has worked inside some of the world's largest AEC firms. She brings her hands-on experience to this book.

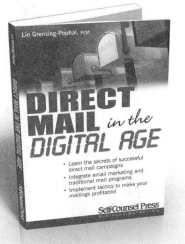

Direct Mail in the Digital Age

Lin Grensing-Pophal, PCM
ISBN: 978-1-77040-071-9
6 x 9 • paper • 168 pp.
First edition
$18.95 USD/CAD

The saturation of email and digital marketing means that as a small business, you must be armed with effective marketing tactics to capture your customers' attention. The author explains why direct mail is an effective tool, and compares direct mail to other marketing possibilities. Small-business marketers will learn to plan a cost-effective direct mail strategy which will pack a punch in their marketing campaign. Author Lin Grensing-Pophal covers topics such as:

- Ensuring the success of your existing direct mail campaigns

- Cost-effective tips for planning and executing direct marketing campaigns

- Making direct mail campaigns work in harmony with other marketing, such as email

- How direct mail is more personal now that almost everything is digital

- — And more!

The Author

Lin Grensing-Pophal has written many business and employee management articles for general and trade publications, and is the author of several books published by Self-Counsel Press. She is accredited through the International Association of Business Communicators and the Society for Human Resource Management, and is a member of the American Society of Journalists and Authors.

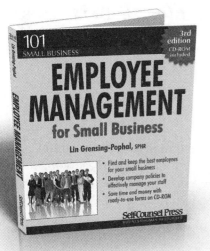

Employee Management for Small Business

Lin Grensing-Pophal, SPHR
ISBN: 978-1-55180-863-5
8¼ x 9¾ • paper + CD-ROM • 200 pp.
Third edition
$20.95 USD/$23.95 CAD

Whether a business has 1 or 100 employees, *Employee Management for Small Business* provides the tools and knowledge required to take an active and positive approach to maintaining an effective human resources plan.

Finding and keeping good employees is crucial to the success of every business, but it's not easy. From hiring and orientation to developing company policies and negotiating employment contracts, this book covers the essentials of employee management.

Like all the books in the *101 for Small Business* series, each topic in the book is explained in simple language and is illustrated with real-world examples, checklists, and forms.

The Author

Lin Grensing-Pophal has written many business and employee management articles for general and trade publications, and is the author of several books published by Self-Counsel Press. She is accredited through the International Association of Business Communicators and the Society for Human Resource Management, and is a member of the American Society of Journalists and Authors.

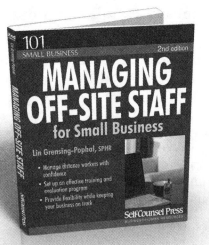

Managing Off-site Staff for Small Business

Lin Grensing-Pophal, SPHR
ISBN: 978-1-55180-865-9
8¼ x 9¾ • paper • 192 pp.
Second edition
$19.95 USD/$21.95 CAD

Does your business need more employees but you don't have the office space to accommodate them? Do you want to promote a flexible work environment, but fear losing profits? Off-site staff may be the answer.

The changing face of today's workplace means that employers need to seek alternative solutions to accommodate the needs of workers, expand their businesses, and attract and keep the best staff.

Managing Off-site Staff provides managers with the tools they need to set up and maintain a productive telecommuting program that benefits both employees and employers.

The Author

Lin Grensing-Pophal has written many business and employee management articles for general and trade publications, and is the author of several books published by Self-Counsel Press. She is accredited through the International Association of Business Communicators and the Society for Human Resource Management, and is a member of the American Society of Journalists and Authors.

Bookkeepers' Boot Camp:
Get a Grip on Accounting Basics

Angie Mohr, CA, CMA
ISBN: 978-1-77040-044-3
8¼ x 9¾ • paper • 204 pp.
Second edition
$18.95 USD/CAD

Bookkeepers' Boot Camp is the first book in the *Numbers 101 for Small Business* series. Demonstrating that precise record keeping and organized financial data are crucial to a business's success, the author gives small-business owners a greater understanding of bookkeeping and a deeper appreciation of it in their businesses.

Hundreds of small-business owners ignore the importance of record keeping and put it off until "later." They end up buried under piles of papers, overwhelmed by the immensity of the task at hand. This book helps these business owners avoid procrastination and unnecessary stress.

The Author

Angie Mohr is a chartered accountant and certified management accountant residing in Savannah, Georgia, USA. Mohr is also a business columnist for a large daily newspaper and has written many articles for business magazines as well as these other books from Self-Counsel Press:

- *Finance & Grow Your New Business*
- *Financial Management 101*
- *Start & Run a Bookkeeping Business*